HOW MAY I HELP YOU?

Providing Personal Service in an Impersonal World

HOW MAY I HELP YOU?

Providing Personal Service in an Impersonal World

Stephen C. Broydrick

IRWIN
Professional Publishing
Burr Ridge, Illinois
New York, New York

Sponsoring editor: *Cynthia A. Zigmund*
Project editor: *Denise V. Santor*
Assistant production manager: *Jon Christopher*
Designer: *Laurie Entringer*
Art Coordinator: *Mark Malloy*
Typeface: *11/14 Times Roman*
Printer: *Book Press, Inc.*

Library of Congress Cataloging-in-Publication Data

Broydrick, Stephen C.
    How may I help you? : providing personal service in an impersonal
world / Stephen C. Broydrick.
        p. cm.
    Includes bibliographical references and index.
    ISBN 1-55623-989-0
    1. Customer service—Automation   I. Title.
HF5415.5.G44 1994
658.8'12'0285—dc20   93-13572

Printed in the United States of America

1 2 3 4 5 6 7 8 9 0 BP 0 9 8 7 6 5 4 3

To Bibs
De Colores!

Preface

There was a time when the only tools of the customer service trade were people skills. The age of automation brought startling changes to the way customers interact with a business. Today's computers process customer information in nanoseconds. Credit or debit card approvals are processed in the time it takes you to read this sentence. Technology is being used to save time for both the business and the customer.

Unfortunately, many businesses have allowed technology to control the way their business is conducted. People skills, so important in a bygone era, have been shunted. Longstanding, loyal customers are left to reminisce about the days when doing business meant enjoying the company of other people. Before anyone noticed, we had become a society of button pushers.

In his book, *Finding the Right Prescription*, Jack Eckerd waxes nostalgic: "Before World War II, the shop owner lived in his community and was a neighbor to his customers . . . his customers came into the store, told him what they needed and he got it for them."[1]

Today, you'll probably find it yourself. In search of aspirin, you might look for a clerk behind the register. Finding no one, you approach a touch screen with a store directory. A synthesized voice announces, "Aisle 26B." By the time you find the aspirin, you really need them.

Tomorrow's successful businesses will have personality, recognizing that the most important resource is the human resource. They'll conclude that providing time-saving technology is not enough. It must be blended with a courteous, personable staff.

As time passes, more and more routine customer service transactions will be conducted through electronic or mechanical interaction. The advent of the automated teller machine (ATM) serves as a precursor of changes to come. Up until the 1970s, all banking was conducted face to face. Gradually, customers warmed to the idea of approaching a machine to deposit or withdraw cash. It is only when the machine ceases to function or "eats" the customer's card that dealing with a person becomes necessary.

A customer's future contact with a customer service representative will gradually be narrowed to those situations where something has gone wrong: a confusing or inaccurate bill, a delay in receiving an ordered product or service, or the breakdown of either hard or soft goods.

Such exceptional situations will call for exceptional people—individuals who possess a strong commitment to serve the needs of others. Tomorrow's customer service representative will cut through the veneer of a customer's anger and dig for solutions that create long-term satisfaction. Technology may come and go, but the value of common courtesy will endure.

How May I Help You? is a book written for this new era of exceptional service. All members of a customer service organization will find it useful. You'll learn how to combine state-of-the-art technology with old-fashioned service. You'll discover the value of thinking creatively when a customer makes special requests. We'll explore why customers sometimes grow angry over seemingly minor frustrations and what you and your staff can do to remain professional in the face of such emotional outbursts.

A special appendix is included for those who deliver service inside a customer's home. Two chapters are devoted to the needs of interacting with co-workers. The chapter on inside service will cover the most effective ways to use voice mail. You'll also learn how to find and keep good customer contact employees.

The best is saved for last. In the final chapter, "Attitude Makes The Difference," you'll learn how to build the foundation upon which all the other skills rest. The individual who works assiduously to improve her attitude will serve as a beacon of energy and hope for everyone who crosses her path. A positive approach to life and work is the most important skill discussed in this book.

This is not a book to be read, but to be *used*. I've attempted to save you time by packing these pages with practical, useful ideas. No artificial fillers of any kind have been added. I suggest you keep a highlighter in your hand as you read, as it is my intention to make sure you wear out that highlighter. At the conclusion of each chapter, you'll be asked to commit to three practical ideas that you can use to immediately improve the way you interact with customers and co-workers.

A special thanks to all the people who made this project such a pleasure: to my wife and business partner, Paula Broydrick, for her continual input and editing assistance; to Cynthia Zigmund at Irwin Professional Publishing, who gave me the freedom to write the kind of book I thought would most benefit the reader; to Richard Larson at the Massachusetts Institute of Technology, who opened my eyes to why people hate to wait for service and what to do about it; to Dr. Frank S. Arcangelo, for his lifelong friendship and his professional input into the chapter on dealing with co-worker conflicts.

Finally, I'd like to thank all the customer service representatives, technical specialists, and service technicians who over the years have let me watch them work and who patiently answered all my questions. I'm pleased and excited to share their ideas in these pages. They have taught me that school is never out for the professional, that a single individual can inspire customer loyalty, and that serving others is more than a source of financial gain. It is the wellspring of personal pride and purpose.

Stephen C. Broydrick

Table of Contents

Chapter Three
BEING FLEXIBLE

Chapter One

Being Fast

D rive down the main street of any town and you quickly learn the priorities of the people who live there. To your left, you see a sign that says "5 Minute Express Lunch." On the right, it's "10 Minute Oil Change" and "Fax Available." Waiting for anyone or anything is considered a waste of time.

Management consultant Michael Fortino provides a unique perspective on wasted time. He estimates that most Americans spend the equivalent of five years of their lives waiting in lines, two years trying to return telephone calls, and one year searching for misplaced objects.[1] Add this up and you begin to understand why many of your customers wait impatiently for good service.

In two-income households, customers face the strain of balancing work and home. Errands are batched to accomplish them more efficiently. A bank is chosen because it's adjacent to the supermarket. Billing questions are resolved by sandwiching a phone call into a busy workday.

If you could take a detached view of this dilemma, you'd find it amusing. Watch people enter an express checkout lane posted as "eight items or less." They're looking for nine items in the cart ahead of them. As motivational speaker Cavett Robert remarked in a recent talk, "I find myself getting annoyed when I have to wait for the next section of a revolving door."[2]

Your customers want it both ways. Make it fast *and* friendly. The business that delivers personality while saving a customer time will be richly rewarded in the years to come.

WAITING IN LINE

Most customers are willing to wait, but not for five years, as described in Fortino's study. The recommended standard for your business depends on the product or service you deliver.

"The doctor will see you now."

Professor Richard Larson of the Massachusetts Institute of Technology (MIT) has carefully studied the behavior of waiting customers. He's discovered that a customer's patience level is determined by what happens when the wait is over. A couple waiting to check luggage on their honeymoon trip is more patient than the person trying to cash his paycheck on his lunch hour. Larson says your customers will accept a long wait only if you deliver a "big payoff" at the end of the wait.[3] A "big payoff" is:

• A great meal.
• The best movie of the year.
• The scariest roller coaster ride of all time.

Restaurants, movie theaters, and amusement parks are fortunate because they can stretch the wait and still provide customer satisfaction. Your product may not be as delicious, entertaining, or thrilling. But you can adopt some of the ideas used by the masters of wait time.

MAKING TIME FLY

Last summer, my wife, Paula, son Kevin, and I waited one hour in line for "Star Tours"—a less-than-four-minute thrill ride at Disneyland. When our four minutes were over, we agreed it had been worth the wait. Not only was there a big "payoff" at the end of the line, but the Disney people made the wait easier than expected. Here's how:

Motion. A customer on the move senses progress. Disney creates maximum motion by minimizing the number of lines used to feed the ride. Instead of waiting in one of several lines in front of the ride entrance, you wind your way through a single, intricate rope system. The ropes ensure first-come, first-served treatment and are very space efficient. More people wait in less space.

Estimated time of arrival. At certain points in line, Disney has signs indicating the approximate time it will take to travel from that point in line to the front of the line. The waiting customer knows what to expect. We knew from the moment we entered the line that it would take us one hour to travel from the back of the "Star Tours" line to the beginning of the ride.

Mind occupation. Virtually every line at Disneyland crosses back on itself so that you are continually passing the faces of other waiting guests. This chance to "people watch" is a pleasant distraction.

The show before the show. About 20 minutes before you actually board the ride, you enter a world of lights, robots, and simulated announcements for trips departing to distant galaxies and strange new solar systems. You're enchanted and amused. You also forget that you're waiting.

The folks at Disney call this the *pre-show*. Every business that keeps customers waiting should have one. The mind with nothing to do enters a time warp. Five minutes feels like an hour; an hour feels like two.

We conduct an interesting experiment in our seminars. The group is asked to sit quietly and guess when 30 seconds have elapsed. There is nothing to occupy the minds of these seminar attendees; they're just waiting for 30 seconds to end. Hands start going up at the nine-second mark. Most hands have been raised by 20 seconds. Rarely does anyone wait a full 30 seconds to raise his hand. A mind with nothing to do compensates by accelerating its internal clock.

So how is your *pre-show?* What are you doing to occupy the minds of your waiting customers? Even if you're unable to use all of Disney's techniques, the creative possibilities are endless.

Could you place a TV in your lobby or waiting area? At Stew Leonard's Dairy in Norwalk, Connecticut, TV monitors are perched above each checkout line and tuned to The Weather Channel™ during peak periods. The Marriott Hotel at Dulles International Airport has a television set located directly behind the check-in counter to help customers cool their heels.

A few miles away, Wingmasters, a Washington, D.C., chicken take-out restaurant, is offering free samples of its fresh baked cornbread to those customers waiting for their orders.

Over 200 supermarkets have made the wait easier by installing VideO-carts™ in their stores. Each shopping cart contains a handle mounted video display device that entertains shoppers with brief movie reviews, trivia games, and community happenings while they wait to reach the register. Electronic summaries of the day's top news stories are also provided from USA Today. It's a great way to occupy the mind and increase a customer's patience.

Maybe you're not ready to join the electronic shopping cart revolution. Perhaps you could entertain your waiting customers by playing an instructional video pertinent to your product or service.

Many businesses do an excellent job of distracting the children of waiting customers. They test the skills of small hands by providing crayons and coloring books. This idea also works with grownups. At Lombardi's Restaurant in Atlanta, menus are presented along with plain, white paper place mats and a small glass of crayons. If your waiter doesn't respond immediately, you can always play another game of "hangman."

A phone call thats delayed at WordPerfect Corporation automatically switches to the company's internal radio station complete with a live "hold jockey." A hold jockey is one part disc jockey, another part traffic reporter. She plays pleasant music while providing regular updates of estimated times of arrival for phone calls destined for specific support groups.

Some major city banks now offer classical music in their lobbies to soothe the frayed nerves of those attempting lunch hour check cashing. If you don't occupy the minds of your waiting customers to the point of distraction, their minds will dwell on one thing—the wait.

Create a *wait time standard* for your business. Let your customers *and* your staff determine the standard you establish. Customers are the ones who have to wait. Your staff will have to live with the standard.

First, invite some of your local customers to participate in a focus group. Ask them:

- How long is *too* long?
- What could we do to make the wait more pleasant?
- Are other businesses serving you more quickly than we are?
- What are those businesses doing to make the wait shorter or more enjoyable?

Next, ask your staff the following questions:

1. How big a "payoff" do our customers receive once served?
2. If *I* were the customer, how long would *I* be willing to wait for our product or service?
3. How long do customers wait at our competition? Is it longer? Is it shorter?

"Based on these answers, we will strive to serve all customers within _____ seconds/minutes."

Keeping Your Promise

Once your speed guideline is established, the following ideas will help you hit your target:

1. *Know your peak business times, and staff accordingly.* You should examine and measure your activity level by the quarter hour each day of the week and, if necessary, each part of the month. Most businesses with walk-in traffic discover that their busiest period is at the noon hour. Have a full staff available during that hour. Schedule employee lunches *before* noon and *after* 1:00 PM. Few things are more annoying to a customer than listening to her own empty stomach growl while hearing an employee behind the counter say, "I'm going to lunch."

Businesses with high telephone volume often discover a "spike" in calls between 9:45 AM and 10:45 AM. Working customers are calling during their morning break. This may be the same time period used for *your* employee breaks. Such alignment can be a roadblock to meeting your standards.

Consider scheduling breaks *outside* the hour when most businesses schedule breaks.

2. *Have the flexibility to "shift" staff at a moment's notice to wait on customers.* CVS, a New England–based drug store chain, places a small push bell at each cashier station. When there are more than three people in line, the register clerk pushes the bell to signal co-workers that it's time to open another register.

Thanks for Waiting

A customer who is not immediately served should always be greeted with, "Thanks for waiting." Apply this greeting in both walk-up and telephone contact. A wait acknowledged is a wait forgiven.

If all of your telephone calls pass through an automatic call distributor (ACD) and your customers hear a recorded announcement that identifies the name of your business, your greeting should begin with, "Thanks for waiting," instead of the name of your business. The delay created by the ACD should be acknowledged. Stating the name of your business is an unnecessary redundancy.

If a recorded announcement is heard only when all your representatives are busy, your representatives should adjust their greeting to the circumstances. Calls sent directly to a representative should be greeted with the name of the business. When a customer service representative knows the caller has been in queue and has heard a recording, she should change her opening from the name of the company to, "Thanks for waiting."

Express Lane or Breakdown Lane?

Express lanes may seem convenient but they are a prescription for chaos. You have to decide how you'll deal with the person who arrives at the front of the line with more than an express amount of business. Customers who read the signs and play by the rules are certain to be annoyed by this customer who has pulled them into the breakdown lane.

Use a queuing line instead. Queuing lines are the answered prayer of every impatient customer. In a queuing system, all customers form a single line and then proceed to the next available customer service representative. The principal advantage of queuing is that it creates maximum motion. The more customer service stations being fed off this single line, the greater the motion. This, in turn, increases the customer's sense of progress. Queuing is fair. Unlike multiple lines, it eliminates the possibility of a customer being trapped in a slow line. One of the unscientific maxims of waiting in line is that when a customer is in a hurry and switches lines to save time, her new line immediately becomes the slowest line in the store.

Professor Larson at MIT notes that customers place critical importance on what he calls *social justice*. A customer is willing to wait his turn provided all customers are waited on in the order in which they arrive.[4]

Queuing lines work with as few as two customer service windows. Simply place a sign on a stanchion that says, "Please wait here for the next representative." Expect a few bumpy days while your customers adjust. Both you and your customers will find the change worthwhile.

Customers should be queued in post offices, banks, airline baggage check-in counters, and payment centers. Queuing lines are more difficult to use where customers occupy a large "footprint" of retail space, such as customers pushing shopping carts. A supermarket or warehouse club with queuing lines will lose large amounts of retail space in front of each cash register. Multiple lines may be the only option.

If you do use a multiple-line system, make a diligent effort to maintain social justice. Let's say you need to close one register and open a new one. One of your employees should *escort the customer who has been waiting in line the longest* to the line about to be opened. The easiest person to move is the newest arrival, the customer at the *back* of the line. But the easy way isn't the fair way. It's not fair to those customers who have been waiting longer.

Employees opening a new register should be taught to ask, "May I help *the next person in line?*" rather than "May I help someone?" The latter question shows a disregard for the concept of social justice. Some Johnny-come-lately customer will undoubtedly try to vault into pole position. Other customers grow irritated with both this customer and your business.

Take a Number

This is a fair, stress-reducing system utilized by many take-out businesses. Once a person takes her number, she breathes a sigh of relief. She knows she'll be waited on before the next person to enter the store. She also can literally "get out of line." Not being anchored to a line will create a more relaxed visit.

The key to a successful take-a-number system is that *all customers take a number*. Set a guideline for how many customers must be waiting before the number dispenser is used. It should be located at the entrance and be hard to miss.

WALK-UP TRAFFIC

Some customer service representatives juggle the needs of front-counter customers and customers calling on the phone. Who should take priority?

The customer who visits your office has invested more time than the customer on the telephone and therefore deserves to be served first. Inform your telephone customer that you are presently with another customer. With the exception of emergencies, offer the telephone customer the options of either holding or having a representative call her back. If you have an open office space where employees seated at their desks are easily seen by walk-in customers, you have two choices:

1. Decide that any employee who is not on the phone will get up and wait on a customer.
2. Block your customers' view of employees.

The customer who is simultaneously waiting in line and watching an employee sitting at his desk is justified in thinking, "Why doesn't he get up and wait on me?"

SETTING EXPECTATIONS

When will I receive my order? When will you call me back? When can I expect that to be repaired? When will the doctor see me? Your chances of satisfying your customer are determined more by the accuracy of your response than the speed with which you deliver your product or service. Customers' expectations are a blank slate. They wait for you to write on the slate. Imagine that you and I both check into a hotel. We both order room service. Both of our meals arrive in 25 minutes. You're a satisfied customer. I'm dissatisfied. When you called room service, you were told your meal would arrive in 30 minutes. When I called, I was told my meal would show up in 15 minutes. Your expectations were met, mine were not. The same level of service created very different levels of satisfaction. You were given accurate information; I was the recipient of wishful thinking.

Notice who set the expectations. In most cases, customers don't set expectations, service providers do. The secret to creating a forgiving customer is:

- *Give it to them straight.* Don't make a promise that will be broken. A customer would rather expect a delay than be surprised by one.
- *Give it to them often.* Provide constant updates. A customer wants to be kept informed, not kept in the dark.

HANDLING PHONE CALLS

Your telephone calls should be answered within 20 seconds. Simple common sense should provide this phone answering standard. If you were calling a friend at home tonight, how many times would you let the phone ring before you were convinced he wasn't home? Four rings? Five rings? Why shouldn't the same standards apply to your business? This means the customer should be speaking to a problem solver within four rings.

If your phone is not answered within this 20-second standard, some customers will act like you're not home and hang up. By 30 seconds, the number of calls abandoned jumps precipitously. Such call abandonment is postponed only if:

- You have no competition.
- The customer's need is so great that it's vital the call be completed.
- You, not the customer, are paying for the call.

Many companies proudly point to their telephone reports showing that 80 percent of their calls are answered within 20 seconds. But who's answering the call? Is it a human being or a machine?

Your customers want to speak to a human being, not listen to a recording. Most customers will "make a selection from the following menu of options," but a customer with a pressing need isn't interested in pressing buttons.

The owner of a telephone store in Portland, Maine, has two equally good suppliers. He has both suppliers' phone numbers programmed as speed dial numbers on his telephone. When he needs supplies, he dials the first supplier. If he hears a recorded announcement, he hangs up and calls the second supplier. On any given day, his business goes to the first company whose phone is answered by a human being.

Automatic Call Distributors (ACD)

An ACD is a device that routes telephone calls and acts like an electronic version of a queuing line. Think of it as a funnel, wide at the top as it accepts calls, and narrowing as it sends calls to whomever is free to serve the customer.

This device is usually paired with a recording informing the customer that he will be served by the next available representative.

Automatic call distributors should be used only to contribute to the speed or fairness with which a customer will be served. An ACD should *not* be viewed or used as a mechanical doorman, greeting every customer who arrives. A customer should hear a recording only if:

• All representatives are busy. During peaks, an ACD helps ensure that one phone caller does not sneak in front of another. Every mid- to large-size business should have an ACD with a recorded announcement for peak periods and then work like crazy to render it unnecessary.

• A business does not have direct-dial phone numbers for individual company employees. A caller can receive recorded instructions to enter the extension number of the employee she'd like to reach. This allows the caller to bypass the switchboard operator and receive faster service.

• The customer prefers to hear a recording. Your company might offer attractive automated services. Some customers call to obtain basic account balance information or verification of a payment, or to place a straightforward order and can accomplish their business most quickly by entering information on the Touch Tone® pad of a telephone.

Info, Not Promo

While your customer is waiting, he could learn more about your company. You could announce recently expanded hours of operation, introductions of new products or store locations, or an enhancement of an existing product or location. Many businesses who extend their office hours are disappointed when so few customers take advantage of the new hours. Customers can't call if they don't know.

You might provide a company telephone directory. For example, your announcement might say, "While you're waiting, you might want to jot down these phone numbers of our other departments." Perhaps your customer misdialed and actually wants to speak to someone at one of the just-announced departments. He can hang up, redial, and save some time. No one likes to wait until he reaches the front of a line to be informed he is in the wrong line.

What could a customer have ready to speed the service she'll receive—an account, invoice, or job number? Ask her to have it in front of her so she can assist your customer service representative. The goal is to occupy the mind of your waiting customer while helping her make efficient use of the waiting time.

One of our clients, a major software developer, uses on-hold time to offer a recording that answers the most commonly asked questions about their products. Frequently, the customer support representative will pick up the call and hear the customer say, "I think your recording just solved my problem."

There are certain no-nos for on-hold time. Do not announce, "Your call is important to us." The customer thinks, "If my call is so important, why am I on hold?" Don't boast about your outstanding customer service. Again, your customer is tempted to talk back to the recording. And don't try to hard sell a customer who is on hold. Having to wait probably lessens the chances of her being in a buying mood.

Here are some samples of effective opening recorded announcements:

> Thank you for calling ACME Explosives. We apologize for the delay but all of our representatives are busy assisting other customers. Please stay on the line and the next available representative will be happy to serve you. We're pleased to announce our new expanded office hours. We're now here every Saturday from 8:00 AM to 5:00 PM. to meet all of your explosive needs. Thank you for your patience.

> You have reached the DOS and Windows support group of ACME software. All of our support specialists are presently assisting other users. Please hold and the next available support person will be happy to answer your questions and help you solve any problems you might be experiencing. Thank you for your patience.

An opening announcement should only be played once. Repeating it over and over is a nagging reminder to the customer that your service is less than the best. Fill the rest of the on-hold time with music, intermittent announcements of useful information, or a combination of the two.

Here are some sample intermittent announcements:

"In order that we may serve you more quickly, please have your account number ready for our customer service representative. Your account number can be found in a shaded box in the upper left-hand corner of your statement."

"Just a reminder that you have reached the support group for the DOS and Windows version of our product. If you're using the Macintosh version, please call 1-800-555-4321. That's 1-800-555-4321. Thank you."

The most appreciated intermittent announcement includes an estimated time of arrival:

"Based on our present pattern of phone calls, we estimate that your call will be answered within the next three to five minutes."

Make an estimate only if you have the estimating technology at your disposal. Be accurate or conservative. Don't make promises you can't keep.

Music on Hold

Recorded music assures a holding customer he has not been cut off. No musical style will satisfy everyone. Avoid music that appeals to only your youngest or oldest customers. Rock will send Grandma through the ceiling; easy listening will put Junior to sleep. Light, upbeat classical or contemporary jazz seems to work best.

Automated Response Units

An automated response unit (ARU) is a customer-assisted call routing system. Its benefits include:

- The ability to handle many more calls than a live switchboard operator.
- The reporting of call counts for various departments. It can help a business determine where it needs to add or trim staff.
- Allowing a business to use a single phone number to serve many different customer needs.
- Permitting a customer to choose between using automated services and speaking to a human being.
- Providing a company with a way to disseminate a vast array of use ful information without human interaction. This frees customer service representatives to focus on customers with special needs.

Some businesses have fully embraced ARU technology. Others are watching and waiting. Here are the arguments *against* ARUs:

• A business loses its human touch. Its first impression is mechanical, not human.
• Typing numbers on a telephone touch pad is awkward, punching letters is annoying; doing either is impossible for customers with rotary dial phones.
• Call count information is inaccurate because customers tend to make an early selection just to leave the menu.
• Customers prefer that the business, not they, perform the telephone routing function.

If your company has made a substantial investment in ARU technology, use these ideas to maximize your investment:

• Ask your customer to push one as soon as possible. This helps divide your Touch Tone® and rotary dial customers. If the ARU doesn't hear a tone in five seconds, the call should go to a switchboard console. This saves a rotary dial customer from listening to all of the various menu options.
• If you offer automated services through your ARU, make those the *first* option. If speaking to a customer service representative is the first Touch Tone® option, no one will wait long enough to discover you offer automated services.

Walking by automation. If you believe your customers will appreciate the time saved by using your automated services, make them "walk by" those automated services each time they call. You'll be borrowing a page of experience from the banking industry.

During the 1970s, banks pleaded with customers to use automatic teller machines (ATMs). It wasn't advertising or promotion that eventually made the machines popular—it was positioning. Smart bankers began placing these machines in the front vestibule of the branch. You couldn't enter the lobby without seeing this small wall with push buttons. On a given Friday, a customer might see a long line and decide to experiment with his shiny new piece of plastic.

Today, banks provide the perfect marriage of people and technology. If your need is routine, head for the machine. If your need requires human interaction, just step into the lobby and speak to a human being. Your phone calls should be handled in a similar fashion.

• Limit the customer's options to three. Don't expect a time-pressed person to listen to, "If you'd like the hieroglyphics department, press 9." You'll know you have too many options on your menu if one of the options is to replay the menu.

Instead, create a set/subset design. For example, let's say you run an insurance company. Your present ARU might say:

- "If you are calling about a personal lines underwriting question, press 1."
- "If you are calling about a commercial lines underwriting question, press 2."
- "If you are calling about an automobile claim, press 3."
- "If you are calling about a fire claim, press 4. . . . "

On and on it goes. You're taking too much of the customer's time without occupying her mind.

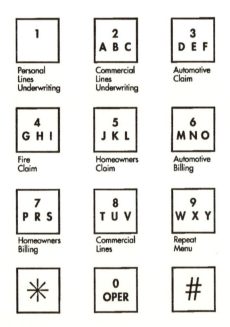

Instead, try it this way:

- "For all underwriting questions, press 1 now."
- "For all questions about claims, press 2 now."
- "For all billing questions, press 3 now."

Notice the use of the words *all* and *now*. *All* is a verbal cue to your customers that they're making inclusive department choices and don't have to wait for half a dozen more choices. *Now* will speed the button pushing process.

Once one of these three options is selected, the customer makes another set of choices. The key is to involve the customer in the call by quickly requesting him to make simple, broad choices.

Let's say your customer has a question about his homeowner's claim. He presses 2 to access the claims choices. *Now* the ARU asks,

- "For automobile claims, press 1 now."
- "For homeowners claims, press 2 now."
- "For all other claims, press 3 now."

Again, he would select 2.

You're doing it this way:"

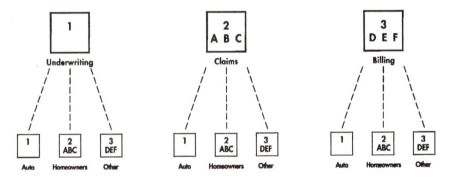

It provides quick entrance into the system. The sooner a customer can push a button, the more receptive he will be to the system. You always want your customer watching, thinking, and doing, instead of simply waiting.

Recording with personality. Pitney Bowes, a supplier of postal, electronic, and mechanical office equipment, uses both a man and a woman on its customer service automated response unit. The woman's voice offers the first menu selection, the man announces the second, and so on. The menu announcements are easier on the ear and create twice the personality of most ARU announcements.

Though many companies hire professional talent to record their announcements, it isn't necessary. Look for two of your employees who possess naturally energetic voices and ask them to do the recording. Your customers hear plenty of polished voices on radio and television. The people recording your announcements should sound like they work at your business, not in a recording studio.

Other Options

If you haven't yet installed an automated response unit to interact with all of your customers, here are some options you should consider:

• Create a separate phone number for each of the departments you were considering consolidating under a single ARU. This allows a customer to speak directly with a human being without pushing buttons.

• Use an ARU to provide automated services only. Establish a separate dedicated phone number for this purpose. Those who wish to use or experiment with automated services will have the option. Offer the customer an easy exit out of the system to reach a switchboard operator.

• Cross-train your staff and offer "one-stop shopping." The customer service representative can handle all of the customer's needs without the need to transfer the call. Nothing leaves a positive first and last impression like dealing with a helpful, versatile human being.

High Tech—No Touch

Businesses thrive when they're customer driven, and stumble when they're technology driven. A wise technology decision saves the company money while saving the customer time. A foolish decision saves the company money while driving the customer up the wall. The most effective advances in customer service technology are hidden—those that speed service but go unnoticed by your customers.

For example, a properly used automatic call distributor isn't a chatty imposition; it's a silent servant. It rushes calls to the next available customer-service representative and maintains social justice.

Some companies use automatic number identification (ANI) technology in a similar behind-the-scenes way. An inbound caller's phone number can be identified and tied to the company's computer. A full customer profile is delivered to the customer service representative moments before he answers the call. In both cases, the technology serves as a tool of faster service without intruding on the way a customer interacts with the business.

WordPerfect Corporation consistently ranks at the top of its field in customer satisfaction. Their philosophy is to create direct personal contact in every telephone call. Each support group has its own phone number, eliminating the need for an automated response unit. The customer's button pushing is limited to dialing the appropriate toll-free number. WordPerfect's only use of ARU technology is its job hotline.

M. Douglas Ivester, president of Coca-Cola USA, puts it bluntly, "We feel that 'press one' technology has no place in a consumer affairs environment . . . consumers, especially those with a problem, should speak immediately with someone who can help them." Ivester goes on to say, "An automated response unit can work well in a promotions environment. It provides consumers with a fast, efficient method of participating in a company's promotion."[5]

Federal Express, recipient of the Malcolm Baldrige Award for service quality, has also shied away from ARUs. Only high-volume customers who prefer automated order pick-up are interacting with this technology. All customer service calls are answered directly by a customer service representative.

800 Numbers

Toll-free numbers are the fastest way to create customer contact. They can be published in owners' manuals, printed in magazines, and announced on the radio. A number used in radio advertising should be memorable because the prospective customer will probably wait until later to place the call. She can't dial a number she can't remember.

This is where clever use of the alphabet can help. Holiday Inns uses 1-800-HOLIDAY. National Car Rental is 1-800-CAR-RENT. Some numbers are humorous. Stanford University's football ticket office is 1-800-BEAT-CAL. If you live in New England and want to learn to square dance, you can dial the New England Square Dancers Information Line at 1-800-33-DO-C-DO.

Clever letters help memory retention but are much harder to dial than numbers. Always provide the numerical equivalent in all your print, radio, and television advertisements. You'll save your customers some time and some irritation.

Speed at A Cost

Some large companies use two methods to ensure customers are served quickly: forced call entry and talk time standards.

In a forced call entry system, a telephone representative receives the next caller in his ear as soon as he completes the existing call. The process is automatic. No wasted time. No unnecessary delays. No sense of control.

Countless scientific studies indicate that people encounter great stress when they feel they have little or no control over their working environment. Rick Gilkey, an associate professor of organizational behavior at Emory University's School of Business Administration, points to research conducted with race car drivers. These daring men and women feel less stress behind the wheel at 200 miles per hour than while at a dead stop in the pits. Out on the track, the driver's in control. In the pits, he's at the mercy of his crew.[6]

Forced call entry places your employees at the mercy of your customer's behavior. What if the most recent caller was particularly rude? Will your telephone representative be at her best with the next caller? Our interviews with present and former customer service representatives make it clear that the forced call entry does save time—but at a price.

Every phone system designed for forced call entry should include a button that permits a customer service representative to enter an *unavailable status*. Customer service representatives should have the freedom to push the unavailable button if they're not emotionally prepared for the next call. Even if rarely utilized, this sense of control over working conditions is a psychologically important exercise of power.

Some companies attempt to speed answer time by creating strict length-of-call or *talk time* standards. For example, one major airline sends its sales offices talk time standards monthly. Sales agents are expected to average no more than three minutes on the phone with each customer. If managers see an agent repeatedly exceeding the standard three minutes, the employee hears about it.

Other companies are taking a more enlightened approach. In 1989, Bell Canada conducted a six-month experiment. Instead of monitoring individual employees, Ontario operators were monitored as a group. Management also stopped disciplining employees whose average talk time exceeded company standards. Carol M. Stephenson, Bell Canada's head of operator services, explained, "If we see a problem with the group average, we ask employees if they know the cause and work with them to get it back down."

The experiment was a success. Nearly 70 percent of the 2,400 operators who participated said their service improved, and 75 percent indicated higher levels of job satisfaction. Thanks to the pilot program, all 5,000 Bell Canada operators now work this way.[7]

It's impossible for your people to simultaneously provide the fastest and the friendliest service. The fastest possible service is rushed service. Customers' questions will go unasked. Employees' answers will be incomplete. Stress levels will rise.

Ironically, the fastest service also wastes more time than it saves. Additional phone calls and visits are required to complete the business that was rushed in the first place. The fundamental error is that you're asking your people rather than your technology to generate speed. Use technology to quickly deliver necessary information to your employees and let your employees concentrate on creating and maintaining rapport.

You'll learn how to build that rapport in the next chapter.

Here are the three ideas from this chapter that I will use right away:

1. _____

2. _____

3. _____

Chapter Two

Being Friendly

Being personable never goes out of style. As more business transactions are processed by machines and computers, customers expect businesspeople to behave more like people, and less like their mechanical or electronic counterparts. What is being friendly? It's handling a customer's needs in a way that motivates him to come back and do business with you again. It's warmth—a sense that if I knew you, I'd like you. It's all the attributes that a man or woman possesses that machines never will:

- A pleasant, responsive manner of speaking.
- A ready sense of humor.
- An adaptability to a person's special need or request.

T.G.I. Friday's restaurants know the recipe for success calls for more than just food ingredients. You can't forget to add friendly, helpful people. New waiters and waitresses are taught a simple but powerful way to assure customer satisfaction. The server has a single goal—to create a *plus* with every customer. Dan Scoggin, former chairman of the restaurant chain, advocated that the waiter or waitress imagine each customer exiting the restaurant with one of three possible impressions—a *plus*, a *zero*, or a *minus*. The *plus*, or positive impression, virtually guarantees that the customer will be back for more. If the customer leaves with a *zero*, or neutral impression, he may or may not return. If he exits with a *minus* or negative, he's gone for good.[1]

Customers always fill out a mental comment card. The impression etched in the mind determines whether the customer will return. This process is continual. Every time the customer deals with your business, a new impression is left, and each new impression is more important than the impressions that came before.

It is the last impression that matters most. Most customers don't care how you have served them in the past. More than any other factor, their decision to return is based on the most recent contact with you and your people. Leave a plus and watch your business grow. Leave a neutral and fertilize the soil for new, aggressive competition. Leave enough minuses and you'll go out of business.

Just providing a great product or service does not guarantee a positive impression. A restaurant's great food can be offset by an unskilled or unpleasant waiter. A company's superior technical support staff can have all the answers, but can make the customer feel like a dodo for asking the questions.

Positive impressions are the result of skillfully blending speed, quality, and personality. Let's make sure your next impression is your very best impression.

BUILD A BUSINESS SANDWICH

Every effective interaction with a customer is broken into three parts:

1. A friendly greeting.
2. Business conducted with continuous rapport.
3. A friendly exit.

Think of the friendly greeting and friendly exit as the top and bottom buns of a "business sandwich." The business is served in between. Without the bun, you leave no better than a neutral impression. It's strictly business.

A friendly greeting creates the rapport. That rapport can be maintained throughout the business. A friendly exit also serves a crucial role. Customers remember the last thing you say or do. More than the other two parts of the sandwich, your last impression drives the customer's decision to do business with you again.

GREETING WALK-IN CUSTOMERS

Most airlines position flight attendants at the gate during the boarding process. Their job is twofold—to pull passenger tickets and to provide a friendly greeting. Airlines know this greeting reassures nervous travelers and establishes a pleasant tone for all the passengers about to make the trip.

Retailers have discovered the value of making the first impression a personal impression. Tom Coughlin, senior vice president of Sam's Clubs, relates the following story in *Sam Walton: Made in America*:

Back in 1980, Mr. Walton and I went into a Wal-Mart in Crowley, Louisiana. The first thing we saw as we opened the door was this older gentleman standing there. The man didn't know me, and he didn't see Sam, but he said, "Hi! How are ya? Glad you're here. If there's anything I can tell you about the store, just let me know."[2]

Sam Walton thought this was one of the best ideas he'd ever seen. After much cajoling and impassioned persuasion, he convinced his managers that every one of their stores should have a people greeter. Walk into any Wal-Mart today and chances are you'll be greeted by someone like that older gentleman from that small town in Louisiana.

The larger the size of your retail store, the more valuable a greeter will be. Customers walking into a vast space can be overwhelmed and made to feel slightly insignificant. Seeing the warm smile of another human being helps provide some needed perspective. Hechinger Company's Home Quarters (HQ) discount hardware stores position an employee just inside the front door to greet customers as they pass through the entrance.

The Towson Town Center, a large shopping complex, helps its customers cope with the overwhelming scale of stores and floors by positioning shopper guides throughout the mall. "We're approached by vendors trying to sell us automated directories but we think our customers appreciate being able to interact with a human being and get their questions answered," says the center's marketing director, Diane Lewis.[3] The shopper guides can direct, or even escort, a newcomer to just the right store to meet his need.

The Olive Garden, an Italian restaurant chain operated by General Mills, Inc., trains employees to open the front door for customers at both the time of entrance and exit. The restaurant is leaving the best possible first and last impression by treating each customer like a guest in a friend's home.

THE POWER OF TOUCH

Nothing creates a better first impression than a firm, professional handshake. It's no accident that politicians develop calluses on their palms. A handshake is the one professional way to use the power of touch.

Imagine you're in the reception area of a doctor's office waiting for your appointment. Almost an hour passes. A nurse approaches the waiting area and calls out your name. You stand up. The nurse gives you a cursory glance, turns her back and says, "Follow me, please."

On your next visit, a different nurse is on duty. She approaches the waiting area and calls out your name. You stand up and the nurse approaches you. She extends her hand and says, "Good morning. My name is Natalie Brooks, an R.N. on staff here. I'll take you back to the exam room. Would you follow me, please?" You begin to feel better before you see the doctor.

Handshakes are an expression of self-assurance and consideration. A hand should be extended with confidence, and you should shake the customer's hand with some gusto. Make it firm. It's better to offer no handshake than a fishy handshake.

Even if a handshake is inappropriate in your circumstances, you should still make the effort to provide a friendly greeting to every walk-in customer. A simple, pleasant "Good morning" or "Good afternoon" works just fine. If you are waiting on one customer and another customer walks into your retail space, politely excuse yourself from the first customer and say to the second, "Good morning, I'll be with you as soon as I can." When it's not possible to greet a waiting customer, he can still be acknowledged. Make eye contact. This is a silent way of saying, "I know you're here. I know you're waiting."

THE SWITCHBOARD

A friendly, professional switchboard operator is one of a company's most valuable assets. He provides a voice and personality to an otherwise large, impersonal business. The right person at the console not only serves every friendly greeting but can also inspire customer loyalty.

Author and management consultant Tom Peters feels that his receptionist, Leslie, is the one who keeps his organization on track. In a newspaper column, "Ode to the Leslies," Peters says that Leslie offers a reminder

> . . . of what an enormous difference one person can make to the spirit of an organization; that energy and enthusiasm really are "everything" and have little to do with job title; that the receptionist is probably the most important person in your company, in terms of external—and—internal tone.[4]

You may never have the chance to write an article about your switchboard operator, but when you find a good one, never let him or her go. Teach the techniques that follow to help your operator or receptionist perform at his or her very best.

Some switchboard operators answer calls this way: "Good morning, International Widgets." This greeting creates switchboard logjams. It also can produce frustration on both ends of the telephone. A first-time caller is forced to guess whether she's speaking to the next available customer service representative or a switchboard operator.

Taking no chances, the caller might begin a long and convoluted description of her need. This necessitates that the switchboard operator interrupt the caller and send her on to someone who can offer assistance. The caller has to explain her situation all over again.

There is a way to dramatically reduce, if not eliminate, these long and involved switchboard sagas. The switchboard operator should answer each call this way: "Good morning, International Widgets. How (or where) may I direct your call?"

This a clear indication to the caller that she is speaking to a gatekeeper, not a problem solver. She's more likely to request a department than to tell a story. It saves both the customer and the switchboard operator time.

Switchboard operators sometimes complain this greeting is too long. On an extremely hectic switchboard console, it is too long. If you must sacrifice part of the greeting, sacrifice the "good morning." "Good morning" is a pleasant, but not a vital part of transferring a call. On an easy day, use all three parts of the greeting. And keep a clock next to the switchboard console. It will prevent your switchboard operators from saying "good morning" at two o'clock in the afternoon.

Pick Up the Phone before You Speak

There are two common mistakes that switchboard operators make that affect a customer's impression of the business: They begin speaking before they answer the call; and they say nothing when transferring the call.

Perhaps you've called a place of business and were unsure if you had reached the right business. Maybe all you heard from the switchboard operator was the final syllable of the business name. "International Widgets" becomes "jets." A law firm with three partners sounds like the sole dominion of the last listed partner. A switchboard operator must make a diligent effort to push the console button before speaking.

The other common oversight is not speaking at all. A caller's request should be acknowledged prior to transferring his call. After making his request to speak to a specific department or person, the customer should hear the switchboard operator say any one of the following: " Just a moment, please," "Certainly," "Thank you," or "I'll connect you." These words convey, "I heard you and will now fulfill your request." If your switchboard operator doesn't acknowledge the request and merely pushes a button, the customer might suspect she's been disconnected.

Placing Customers on Hold

When I worked in Los Angeles, I had an office directly behind the switchboard operator's work space. Our company went through switchboard operators like children go through shoes. The most memorable operator was a temporary employee who could place more calls on hold in less time than the world's most sophisticated automatic call distributor.

If six calls reached the switchboard console at about the same time, she would say *all* of the following in slightly under six seconds: "Spotlight, please hold, Spotlight, please hold, Spotlight, please hold, Spotlight, please hold, Spotlight please hold, Spotlight, please hold." She could answer six calls in the time it takes a telephone to ring once! She would then return to the still dazed first caller and say, "Spotlight, may I help you?"

There is a more pleasant and effective way. Using the same company name, here's the best way to place someone on hold:

- "Good morning,
- Spotlight.
- Will you hold, please?"

Notice this is a request, not a command. The customer should be given an opportunity to respond to the question. "Please hold" is rude. Asking "Will you hold, please?" and not allowing the customer a chance to respond to the question, isn't an improvement.

Three customer responses are possible—yes, no response at all, and no. If the answer is yes, the switchboard operator should say thank you and move on to the next caller. Upon returning to the original call, she should say, "Thanks for holding. How may I direct your call?"

No response to the question, "Will you hold, please?" is caused by catching a customer off-guard. He's surprised to discover a switchboard operator patient enough to wait for a response. If no response is forthcoming, simply repeat the question, "Will you hold, please?" If there is still no response, the customer should be placed on hold. The switchboard operator has an obligation to the other customers waiting to be served.

If the answer is no, the reason for the no should be determined. Perhaps it's the emergency room of a local hospital calling to inform an employee that his son has fallen out of a tree and cannot be treated without parental permission. Such a call takes instant priority over all others.

But there is another type of no. It's the caller who makes it clear that he believes his call should take priority despite the fact that other callers arrived before him. Within the boundaries of the real world of business, social justice should prevail. The fair way to deal with all customers is on a first-come, first-served basis. Only you can decide whether you want to allow certain customers to jump to the front of the line.

Other Telephone Greetings

Each effective telephone greeting should communicate three elements of information:

- *Where* you are.
- *Who* you are.
- You're willing to help the customer—you just need to learn *how* you can be of assistance.

A customer service representative at International Widgets should answer his phone this way:

- "Customer Service.
- My name is Tony.
- *How* may I help you?"

The greeting tells the customer, "You've reached the right place, you're speaking to a human being, and I'm happy to help you. Just tell me *how*." This greeting assumes that either a switchboard operator or a recording has previously told the caller she has reached International Widgets. If this is not the case, the customer service representative should add "International Widgets." There is no good morning or good afternoon in this prescribed greeting. It makes the greeting too long.

Where am I? Make sure your department names are enlightening, not confusing. Some hardware/software divisions answer their phones, "Information Services." A customer might think, "Have I reached the computer department or the public relations area?" An insurance company's claims office might include a personal injury protection (PIP) department. A customer might call and hear, "PIP department, my name is John, how may I help you?" The caller says to herself, "Did I reach the right person or did John once sing with Gladys Knight?"

A customer service representative using his first name generates friendliness. Offering only a last name creates respect and formality. It can also cause confusion. If you have an unusual last name and use it in the greeting, the customer may become distracted by your name rather than focused on his need. Use your last name only if there is more than one employee with your first name in your department and only at the end of the conversation.

First names can be presented in three different ways:

- "This is Tony."
- "Tony speaking."
- "My name is Tony."

"My name is Tony" is the best way. Some of our clients have experimented with these three options and found that a customer is most likely to retain and use a customer service representative's name when it is preceded by "my name is." The customer is receiving a verbal cue that the next word the employee will speak is his name. When you precede your name with "this is," the customer faces a brief moment of suspense.

How is the magic bullet. "May I help you?" is a wide open question. Asking this question is analogous to being a trail guide with no sense of direction. The customer will start down one of several verbal paths meandering as she speaks, providing information that is incidental and makes little contribution to meeting her need.

"*How* may I help you?" provides the customer with a starting point. It's a polite way of saying, "Let's get right to the heart of the matter." It is also an expression of employee confidence. The customer service representative is not querying *whether* he can help, but is asking in what way he can offer assistance. Adding this single short word to an employee's greeting saves countless unnecessary words spoken by the customer.

Holiday greetings. If you call directory assistance in area code 608 between Thanksgiving and Christmas, you might receive a small gift. Your operator might say, "Happy Holidays, what city, please?" The directory assistance operators in this part of Wisconsin are granted artistic license to spread holiday cheer. One operator really shares the spirit. Her holiday greeting is, "Ho, ho, ho, what city please?" Let your staff add a touch of the season as Christmas and Hanukkah draw near.

Not so fast. One final suggestion regarding telephone greetings. Be sure your customer service representatives answer calls at a moderate speaking velocity. Some customer service representatives answer so quickly that you have to record the greeting and play it back at half speed to determine the name of the business and the person answering the call. A greeting makes no sense ifitallrunstogether.

Transferring Calls

A call can be transferred in the following ways:

- A co-worker's extension can simply be buzzed.
- A co-worker can be reached on the intercom and told he has a call on line one.
- A co-worker can be reached on the intercom and told who is calling.

The last option is the *Twinbrook technique.* At the Twinbrook Insurance Agency in Holbrook, Massachusetts, owner Frank Rizzo instructed his switchboard operator to ask each incoming caller, "May I tell her who's calling?" The operator could say, "May I ask who's calling?" but saying it this way makes her sound more curious than helpful. Equipped with the name, she goes to the intercom button, the employee about to receive the call is told the name of the caller, and the transfer is completed.

The customer service representative can now answer:

- "Hi, Mr. Rodriguez,
- this is Shirley.
- *How* may I help you?"

There are two primary advantages for Shirley:

1. She builds better rapport by using her name and the customer's name in the greeting. Nothing is more pleasing to a customer's ear than the sound of his own name.
2. She's never surprised by the voice on the other end. Shirley can pull up Mr. Rodriguez's account before she picks up the phone.

Most switchboard operators don't have the time to offer the *Twinbrook technique,* but it should be used whenever a call is transferred from one department to another. It's an excellent example of internal customer service and is especially appreciated by the customer who has been mistransferred more than once.

CALLING OUT

A customer service representative placing an outbound call should identify himself and his business *before* asking to speak to the customer. It's a pleasant courtesy when calling a customer's place of business and prevents embarrassment when a male employee calls the home of a female customer and a man answers the phone. Similar awkwardness is possible when a female employee needs to reach a male customer at his residence and a female answers the phone.

Tony from International Widgets might call a customer's home and say "Hi, is Mary there?" Mary's husband might respond, "That depends. Who are you?" Tony would be better served by creating this friendly greeting: "Hi, this is Tony from International Widgets. May I speak to Mary?"

SMOOTH TRANSITION INTO BUSINESS

The momentum of rapport created in the friendly greeting should be maintained throughout the business part of the sandwich. Too often, a customer service representative will provide a friendly greeting and move too abruptly into the business and consequently break rapport.

Let's say a customer describes his problem. The customer service representative knows that she can provide no help until the customer's account history is on her computer screen. Wishing to get the problem solved as quickly as possible, she uses the same opening question for every problem: "What's your phone number?"

The customer knows that explaining his problem was a waste of time and that the customer service representative is more interested in getting the call completed than she is in being helpful. Cathy McKee, a trainer for TCI Cablevision in Lincoln, Rhode Island, teaches this effective method of moving from friendly greeting into the business:

- "I can help you with that.
- Could I have your phone number
- so I can pull up your account?"[5]

Notice that the customer's request or problem is being acknowledged with confidence. The account is accessed in a friendly way. Additionally, the customer knows why the phone number is being requested.

Phone numbers are the best way to pull accounts because customers know their phone numbers. This keeps your phone information accurate and updated. If your company uses automatic number identification (ANI) technology, accurate phone numbers are a must. It also saves some customers from spelling their long and unusual names.

What about asking for an account number as part of the telephone greeting? "International Widgets, this is Tony. Could I have your account number, please?"

This greeting gives the impression you're in a hurry and creates an awkward moment for customers who don't have their account numbers available. It also does nothing to build rapport. In all cases, a customer should be allowed to speak *before* the customer service representative pulls up an account.

RAPPORT BUILDERS AND RAPPORT BUSTERS

Information can be solicited in one of two ways: using favor language or command language. *Favor language* is asking questions. *Command language* is giving orders. Favor language helps you gather all the necessary details while maintaining the goodwill you created in the friendly greeting. It's saying: "Could I have your phone number?" "Could I have the address?" "Would you spell your last name?"

Pat from Providence

Pat Scorpio, a creative customer service representative from Rhode Island, shares this idea, "I always try to use favor language when I speak to my customers. But I improve on this concept by adding the words 'for me' whenever I can. Instead of just saying, 'Would you spell your name?' I ask, 'Would you spell your name for me?' It's no longer just a favor. It's become a personal favor."[6]

When asking for any nonmemorized information, either add the word "handy" to the end of your request or begin your request with, "Do you happen to have . . .?" Any possible customer embarrassment at being unprepared is eliminated.

- "Do you have your account number handy?"
- "Do you happen to have the claim number in front of you?"

Command language is a rapport buster. It's treating the caller like a private in basic training rather than a valued customer.

- "Give me your phone number."
- "Spell your last name."
- "What's your address?"

It can be even more efficient:

- "Name?"
- "Address?"
- "Date of birth?"
- "Social security number?"
- "Take a seat."

Aye-aye captain! Command language is most often heard in businesses where employees feel pressed for time and face an endless stream of customers who ask the same questions or look for the same answers. When renting a car, you might approach the counter hoping for a Business Sandwich and instead get indigestion. All you hear is: "Valid driver's license. Major credit card."

I once visited a major department store and asked if I could pay for my purchase with a check. Instead of receiving a yes, no, or an explanation, the response was: "New England driver's license. Major credit card."

I'm sure that many years ago, the cashier's response was more thorough: "Yes, provided that you can show me a driver's license from a state in New England and have a major credit card." Being asked the same question over and over had worn her down.

The late actress Mary Martin was best known for her leading role in the musical Peter Pan. Late in her career, a reporter asked her, "Ms. Martin, I saw your performance tonight and it was so fresh, so new. When you exclaimed, 'I can fly! I can fly!' it seemed like the very first time you had ever said those lines. How do you do it?" Ms. Martin paused, pointed to the now empty seats of the theater and said, "It was the first time for them."[7]

Your next customer may be the 90th person today to ask you the same question. But it's the first time for him. He deserves the same courtesy you extended to the very first customer you ever served. Favor language will help you keep it fresh and make it friendly.

Give 'em the Johnny Most

The second great rapport builder is the "Johnny Most." For 37 seasons, Johnny Most was the radio play-by-play announcer for the Boston Celtics of the National Basketball Association (NBA). He brought each game to life with his colorful descriptions of shots made and fouls missed.

Let's escape into a time tunnel and travel to 1969. You've tuned in to the seventh and final game of the NBA World Championship where the Celtics face the Los Angeles Lakers. All you hear is the noise of the crowd. Johnny's disappeared and you try desperately to determine what's happening on the basketball floor from the wax and wane of the fans' cheers.

That's how it is for your customers. Without a description of what's happening on your end of the telephone, a customer is left in the dark. He relies on your play-by-play announcing skills to shed light on your efforts to solve his problem.

Customer service representatives are most prone to these communication lapses while in front of a computer. The images and information on the screen fully engage the employee's mind. While tuning in to the screen she may unintentionally tune out the customer. She must master the customer service equivalent of walking and chewing gum at the same time.

Rapport is maintained by looking and speaking simultaneously: "Let me see if I can find what we're looking for on this next screen. This will just take me a second. No, I don't see it there. We'll probably find it on this last screen. Yes, there it is."

Here's another example of giving the Johnny Most: "What's just come up on my terminal is a blank lost order report. I'll ask you some questions and we'll fill in this report together."

Leaving a telephone breaks rapport. It can only be maintained during the interruption by providing the Johnny Most: "The person who has the answer to that question works about 20 feet from here. Would you be willing to hold while I walk over and ask him?" The customer can now form a mental picture of the situation on your end of the telephone. Cooperation and rapport are maintained.

The best rapport is created when a customer service representative uses personal pronouns: "Here's what *I'm* going to do . . ." or "Why don't *we* try this . . ." *We* indicates a willingness to form a two person team and is a wonderful way to build warmth and confidence through a telephone wire.

The Johnny Most can be used by anyone who has a customer. A cab driver can briefly describe the route he'll take to get his passenger to her destination. A physician conducting a physical examination can let the patient know what she'll do next and describe any pain that can be expected. Repair technicians and carpenters who are constantly in and out of a home can put customers at ease by informing them where they're going and when they'll be back. The Johnny Most is a rapport builder. Silence is a rapport buster.

Sharing the Screen

Lack of eye contact in face-to-face transactions is another rapport buster. You may become so glued to a computer terminal that you appear more interested in the screen than in the customer. Additionally, the customer can grow frustrated that you're looking at information about him that he can't see. Rotate your terminal so that both you and the customer are viewing the information simultaneously.

Radio Shack, a division of Tandy Corporation, angles its point-of-sale terminals so that both the store associate and customer can see the details of the sale. This engages the mind of the customer and helps him to verify or correct his name, current address, phone number, or pricing information at the time of the purchase.

Say It and Type It

When dealing with a customer by telephone, repeat aloud any information you're typing into your computer terminal. This allows a customer to verify or correct the spelling of her name, her address, telephone number, or any other pertinent data before it becomes a permanent part of her customer profile.

MIGHT/REALLY/COULD

During the course of a business conversation, customer-contact employees might say one thing and the customer might hear something quite different. Consider these often used, but misinterpreted, expressions:

- "What can I do for you?"
- "What I'm trying to tell you is . . ."
- "All I can do is . . ." or "The best I can do is . . ."

"What can I do for you?" Filtered through a customer's ear this can sound like, "Hurry up." Take the situation of calling a business, identifying yourself, and then asking the individual on the other end of the line, "How are you today?" "Fine, what can I do for you?" is the response. Your ears don't hear the words spoken but the customer service representative's intent, which is a combination of "Make it snappy" and "Don't try to get friendly with me, buster!"

Might say: "What can I do for you?"
Really saying: "Hurry up."
Could say: "How can I help you?"

"What I'm trying to tell you . . ." This is an expression of exasperation. The customer service representative has made an unsuccessful attempt to provide an explanation and grows weary of explaining a second or third time. The lack of communication is being blamed solely on the customer.

Might say: "What I'm trying to tell you . . ."
Really saying: "You're not very bright."
Could say: "Let me see if I could explain this better."

Offering to try again and explain in a better way is an admission that the lack of communication might be caused by the quality of your explanation, rather than the customer's inability to understand. You've let the customer off the hook.

"All I can do . . ." With a polite and easy-going customer, you would have been willing to bend. Deal with an inflexible customer and you feel yourself responding in a rigid fashion. This customer makes you want to go strictly by the policy manual.

Might say: "All I can do . . ."
Really saying: "You're not going to get what you want."
Could say: "I can't do that, but here's what I can do."

Every customer making special requests should be presented alternatives that might be equally satisfying. It's important not to let a customer's disposition affect your response.

If you supervise a customer service staff, create your own collection of might/really/coulds. As you monitor your employees' interaction with customers, listen for those expressions that might stir the ire of your customers. Share in an informal meeting with your employees what the customer really hears and suggest what your employees could say instead.

THE AT&T IDEA

AT&T offers this excellent suggestion in their telephone skills programs: Give customers two options and position the one you want them to choose as the second option.[8]

For example, suppose it's an extremely hectic day and you would prefer to solve a customer's problem now, rather than taking a name and number and calling the customer back. You would propose the following: "Do you want me to take your name and number and call you back or would you prefer to hold for a moment and see if we can get this resolved now?"

Customers tend to remember the last thing you say or do. Most customers presented with these two options will stay on the line. Maybe your preference is to call the customer back. "Would you like to hold or can I take your name and number and give you a call back?" Most customers will request a callback. The two advantages of the AT&T idea are that your customer is the decision maker and that you are able to influence the decision.

THE FRIENDLY EXIT

The bottom bun of the business sandwich is the part that deepens and so-lidifies the impression left with the customer. The only way to ensure that a customer is completely satisfied with the results of his contact with you is to ask:

- "Is there anything else I can help you with today?"
- "Would you like to order anything else today?"
- "Have I answered your question?"
- "Have I answered all of your questions?"

"Have I answered all of your questions?" convinces your customer that your goal is to deliver total satisfaction. It removes inhibitions and intimi-dation and uproots questions that otherwise might go unasked. It also helps you conduct more business in fewer visits or phone calls. Instead of the customer calling back 15 minutes later and asking more questions, all busi-ness is completed in a single call.

The last words you speak will be the ones most remembered. If you expect the customer will need to follow up with you, offer your name and extension number: "Mrs. Haywood, feel free to call and ask for me. My name is Lois and my extension is 212."

If it's not critical the customer speak to you personally, make the name of your company the last word. "I'm glad I could help, Mrs. Haywood. Thank you for calling International Widgets." Exiting the call with the name of your business helps you leave a positive and lasting impression that's good for your business. You're creating market share in the mind. The next time your customer has a need, he is more likely to call you than your com-petition.

Airline pilots or flight attendants at Delta Airlines often conclude a flight by saying, "We know you had a choice of airlines today and we appreciate your choosing Delta." The last word heard is the name of the airline. When you contact your long distance carrier's operator, notice how he gets in the last word: "Thank you for choosing AT&T," or "Thank you for using MCI," or "Thanks for choosing Sprint."

The business sandwich is complete. The customer service representative can prepare to offer a friendly greeting to the next customer and begin the process once again. But to the true professional, the process is less like assembly-line production and more like creating a work of art.

Elevating customer service to this new level is simply a matter of placing your personality on the line every time. Everybody wins. The customer who deals with a real person is more satisfied and develops a greater sense of loyalty to your business. You'll look in the mirror at the end of the day, pleased with what you see, and proud of what you've accomplished.

Here are the three ideas from this chapter that I will use right away:

1. _____

2. _____

3. _____

Chapter Three

Being Flexible

You're a postal employee in a large city. A customer walks into your post office to pick up his mail. "Oh, I'm so forgetful," he says. "I left the key to my mail box at home. Would you be willing to get my mail for me?"

What would you say?

- "Happy to do that for you, sir. I'll be right back with your mail."
- "United States Postal Code, Article 6324, Section 645B, subsection 7820 states, 'Mail stored in mailboxes shall only be retrieved by the boxholder with said boxholder's key. Any other persons or postal employees touching such mail shall be subject to a fine.'"
- "I'd be happy to get your mail, but for your own protection, could I see some identification that verifies you are the boxholder? I'm sure you wouldn't want me turning over your mail to any stranger who approached me asking for it."
- "I'll have to go check with my supervisor."

Let's say you're a teller at the drive-up window of a bank. A bicyclist rides up to your window. He's come to you because he left his bike lock at home and fears leaving his bike outside the bank while visiting the lobby. He says, "Hi, I'd like to deposit this check." What would you say?

- "You'll have to go inside with that. Didn't you see the sign? No bikes in the drive-up area."
- "Happy to do that. Oh, would you like a lollipop?"
- "I can go ahead and deposit that now. But in the future, you'll have to go into the lobby instead of coming to the window."
- "I wish I could do that out here, but the bank's liability insurance doesn't cover customers on bicycles; so if you were to crash and hurt yourself you could sue us. Our lobby is still open."

Here's one more situation. A customer with his arms full of clothing approaches the customer service desk at the clothing store where you work: "Hi, I'd like to return these clothes and get my money back. I've recently lost 25 pounds and they no longer fit me." What would *you* say?:

- "We would be happy to give you your money back. And by the way, we'll be donating these clothes to charity."
- "Recent medical research shows that 93 percent of all people who take off weight put all of the weight back on. Therefore, I would recommend that you keep the clothes until they fit you once again."
- "I can't give you your money back. These clothes have been worn so we can't resell them. Besides, there's nothing wrong with these clothes."

STAY FLEXIBLE

If you want to improve your competition's business, just say no. Your customers will quickly beat a path to someone else's door. Any business facing competition must remain flexible towards a customer's ever-changing needs. Being flexible means:

- Listening to your customer's special request inclined to saying yes.
- Teaching staff that just saying no is not saying enough. A customer expects and deserves to hear the reason why his request is being turned down.
- Reviewing company policies to determine whether they still make sense. Your staff should be both comfortable in, and capable of, explaining the *why* behind the policy.
- Offering to make an exception to a policy if it helps retain a customer.
- Driving more of the decision making into the hands of the employee who has initial customer contact.

Keeping Your Balance

Exceptional situations force a business to a walk a tightrope. You're tipped in one direction by the desire to say yes so the customer keeps coming back. You lean the other way so can you can remain profitable and prevent "giving away the store."

Consider the situation in the clothing store. It can't afford to give full refunds to every customer who's lost weight. Yet, just saying no risks customer *dis*satisfaction and loss of future business. Each situation challenges the customer contact employee to create a solution that simultaneously satisfies her customer and the person who signs her paycheck.

THE OPTIONS

There are five possible responses to any customer request:

1. No.
2. No, here's why I'm saying no.
3. No, here's why I'm saying no, but here's what I can do for you instead.
4. Yes, I'll do it this time but here's why I can't do it in the future.
5. Yes.

Here are the consequences of each response:

1. *No.* This an unacceptable answer unless you have no interest in ever serving this customer again. If you could look up the word no in a customer's dictionary you'd find, "Go away!"

No is an attitude. It can permeate an organization. It's reinforced by signs that contain the word *no*. Such signs hurl a visual obstacle at the customer and rob your staff of the chance to make a good first impression.

A potential customer pulls up to a convenience store on a busy road in a tourist town. Emblazoned on the front door in large letters a sign reads, "NO PUBLIC REST ROOMS." This is like laying out a welcome mat that says, "SCRAM!" That potential customer trying to answer nature's call quickly takes her need and her money elsewhere.

Five miles up the road, a kitchen supply store on a busy street has on its door, "We gladly make change for parking meters." You might walk in, get your change, be offered a sample of their delicious brewed coffee and walk out with four quarters and two pounds of coffee beans.

If it's necessary to say no, let your people, not words on the wall, do the talking. At Walt Disney Co.'s amusement parks, employees, known as cast members, are trained to deal with guests' extraordinary behavior on a one-to-one basis. Occasionally, a guest will slow down a line at a thrill ride because he wants to occupy an entire row of seats by himself. The cast member would explain to the guest that it's not possible to quickly load the ride if several seats go unused.

A nearby theme park handles the same situation with a sign, "No preferred seating." What does "no preferred seating" mean? Despite the sign, employee intervention will still be necessary. A sign also tempts the employee not to explain, but to simply point at the sign.

If you feel that a sign *is* necessary, consider injecting it with a healthy dose of humor. The San Diego Zoo can't have employees staked out to observe every guest at every moment. Yet they want to ensure that the animals are left undisturbed by these visitors from another civilization. Here's the sign you'll see throughout the park:

"Please do not annoy, torment, pester, plague, molest, worry, badger, harry, harass, heckle, persecute, irk, bullyrag, vex, disquiet, grate, beset, bother, tease, nettle, tantalize, or ruffle the animals."

Mission accomplished. With tongue firmly in cheek, the zoo creates the desired behavior while placing a broad smile across a customer's face.

Balloons at the Hospital

Hospitals around the world have instituted a policy of forbidding mylar balloons in patients' rooms. Two reasons are cited:

- Deflated balloons pose a choking hazard for patients and visitors, especially small children.
- The balloons can block a nurse's path to a patient in the case of an emergency.

What would be the best way to get this message to a hospital's customers? One of our clients has made an impressive transition in the way they say no. When the policy was first established, it was communicated by signs at the reception desk: "No balloons permitted in patient rooms."

Visitors with beautiful bouquets of balloons asked *why*. The answer delivered depended solely on *who* was behind the desk. Employees were guessing. One employee was offering The Wizard of Oz response: "If the helium in those balloons is breathed in by our staff, it could cause health problems." Instead of better understanding the hospital's logic, some visitors might imagine staff skipping down the halls singing, "Follow the Yellow Brick Road."

Step one. The signs were removed. Step two. Staff was provided the correct reason for the balloon ban and taught how to explain it clearly to visitors. Step three. A detailed explanation was printed and offered to any visitor who might arrive with balloons. The hospital also decided to explain the policy in plain English. Instead of using medical terms like asphyxiation and aspiration, they used the word choking.

2. *No, here's why.* This second possible response to a customer's request is a step in the customer's direction. As in the hospital case study above, the customer is told the reason that the request must be turned down. The best explanations often include the word *fair:*

"I wouldn't be able to do this for other customers so it wouldn't be fair if I did it for you."

"What you're asking me to do will cost our company a significant amount of money. We won't be here to serve you if we can't make a fair profit on what we sell."

If you return to the opening three examples in this chapter, you'll see how a "here's why" can be used.

• *Post Office.* "I'm sure that you wouldn't want me turning your mail over to anyone who comes in asking for it."

• *Bank Drive-Up Window.* "We're concerned that automobiles have difficulty seeing pedestrians and cyclists so we've made it a policy to restrict transactions to cars only. We do this for your safety." (Notice the concern for the customer's safety rather than the fear of a lawsuit.)

• *Clothing Store.* "We do offer a satisfaction guarantee on our clothes but it seems you are satisfied with the clothes; they simply no longer fit you. We try to treat all of our customers in the same manner. If I give you a refund, I should really give every customer in a similar situation a refund. To do that would jeopardize our chances of being profitable."

Level with your customers. Profit and fairness are not dirty words. Business relationships are built on a foundation of trust. Worthwhile policies will be accepted by your customers if:

• You show how the policy protects your customer's health, safety, or wallet.
• You appeal to your customer's sense of trust and fair play.

When a Reason Is Not an Explanation

"It's against company policy" is *not* enough. Not only does it say nothing but it may frustrate your customer more than no explanation at all. If you find you or your staff using this phrase instead of offering an explanation, take it as a warning. One of three situations now exists:

1. Your staff doesn't know why your company has the policy.
2. You or your staff are not willing to take the extra time needed to explain why the policy exists.
3. The policy no longer makes sense and no one's taken the time to question it.

3. *No, here's why, but here's what I can do.* Assuming there's a good reason for your policy, this is the best of the five possible responses to a customer's request. You successfully make that walk across the tightrope because you both satisfy the customer and operate a profitable business. Now you're thinking creatively. In addition to explaining your policy, you're searching for an imaginative alternative that *may be as satisfying to the customer as what he initially requested.*

Return again to our opening case studies:

• *Post Office.* "I've never seen you before and I think you'd understand that I wouldn't want to give your mail to just anyone who walks in here asking for it. There are a number of ways I can get you your mail. Do you have two forms of identification, including a picture ID? If not, let me go pull the signature card on this box rental and have you sign your name for me and I'll compare signatures. Or, just to save some time, is there anyone working here this morning who knows you and can vouch for you?"

• *Bank Drive-Up Window.* "There must be a way for you to go inside the bank without worrying about your bike. What if you were to leave it over there where I can see it while I work. That way, I won't be violating our policy and you can get your banking done without worrying about your bike."

• *Clothing Store.* "I think you can see that we can't offer refunds to every customer who loses weight, but *here's what I can do.* I'd be happy to offer you a 50 percent discount on any new purchases you make today and we'll take the clothes you're returning and donate them to a local charity in your name."

The clothing store retains the integrity of its policy, and is willing to sacrifice today's profit to ensure that the customer is motivated to purchase from the store in the future. The customer receives a special kind of satisfaction knowing that his old clothes will find a grateful new owner.

4. *Yes, but here's why I can't next time.* This is saying yes but explaining that the next time the answer will be no. Your goal is to educate the customer so that he'll be aware of the policy in the future. We call this offering a *one waive.*

The *one waive* creates customer satisfaction today and prevents abuse of a useful policy tomorrow. It's not just saying yes. Just saying yes encourages the customer to repeat the request.

Let's return to the clothing store to apply the *one waive*: "Because you weren't aware of the limits of our satisfaction guarantee, I'm going to make a one-time exception to our policy and give you a refund. Please remember that this is an exception, and we won't be able to do this in the future."

The clothing store response illuminates the potential weakness in a *one waive.* There is no assurance that the customer will behave differently the next time he deals with the business. The customer must be persuaded that the policy makes sense or he'll simply make the same request again.

The Credit Card

Imagine a bank credit card company that attracts business by offering their card with no annual fee. They choose to generate profits from the combination of interest charges and by assessing a 2 percent transaction fee on all cash advances.

When prospective customers applied for the card, NO ANNUAL FEE was prominently displayed on the application. By contrast, the 2 percent transaction fee was buried in the terms and conditions.

A customer's card arrives and he decides to get a cash advance for $5,000. All goes well until he receives his credit card statement. To his surprise, there it is—a $100 transaction fee.

He calls the credit card company and says, "If I had known there was going to be a $100 fee for that cash advance, I would have decided to find another way to obtain $5,000. I don't feel I should have to pay this transaction fee."

What could the credit card representative do?

- She could insist that the $100 be paid and use the fine print as her defense.
- She could use a *one waive*, offering to delete the transaction fee this time and making it clear it will have to be paid the next time.
- She could virtually guarantee there will be no waiver next time by noting the exception in the customer's account history.

This last option is known as a *documented one waive*. This allows any customer service representative who subsequently speaks to this customer to be aware of any past exceptions to policy. The next customer service representative makes an informed decision and can reinforce what the customer has been told in the past.

"Mr. Jones, my records show that you called us on April 18 and that our customer service rep both explained our policy and provided a one-time waiver of that fee. This time I'll have to let that charge stand."

A *documented one waive* creates immediate customer satisfaction while virtually guaranteeing that regular policy will be applied in the future.

Although a *documented one waive* is extremely effective, it's also potentially dangerous. If you're documenting every policy exception, you're creating a breeding ground for paranoia. Your staff begins to think all customers should be considered untrustworthy until proven otherwise.

Successful businesses operate with just the opposite philosophy. Each customer is considered *trustworthy* until there's clear reason to think differently.

5. *Yes.* This is clearly the response most likely to bring your customers back. Inflexible employees say, "I can't." Enlightened employees ask, "Why can't I?" If an employee can't think of, or be provided with, a rock solid reason to say no, she should say yes.

If They Point, Follow

Your customer's special requests also provide you the future direction of your business. If you begin hearing the same request from different customers, consider it a very loud knock on your door. Answer it. Your customer's not trying to be difficult. He's escorting you to a new room filled with opportunities to grow and expand your business.

A grocery store manager is approached by an elderly gentleman who asks, "Can I buy a half a loaf of bread?" Some managers would just say no. *This* manager talks to his bread supplier and asks him to create a smaller loaf for those who live alone. The change causes a significant rise in bread sales.

A hospital begins to hear patients ask, "How much will my elective surgery cost?" In the past, the answer has been, "I can't tell you." But the marketing department of the hospital realizes that the patient has options: not only *whether* to have the surgery but *where* the surgery will be performed. Hospital management thinks employees should ask, "Why can't I?" and empowers employees to quote fees. This new approach keeps them one step ahead of the hospital across town.

Federal Express often heard customers say, "It's not important that this be delivered overnight. Could you promise delivery in two days and charge me less?" "Why not?" said Federal Express. The result was a new form of service, economy overnight, which today is a major revenue source for the company.

Consider the credit card company with the sky-high transaction fee. If a multitude of customers are calling to question the fairness of these charges, it's probably time to redesign the product.

Ask your frontline staff. Are many different customers making a single identical request? Have you been saying no? Maybe it's time to find a way to say yes.

EMPOWERING YOUR STAFF

Transforming employees into decision makers requires salesmanship. The benefits of changing must be persuasively presented and all objections directly addressed. Here are the roadblocks you'll face on the path to empowerment:

• *It's easier to say no.* A force must act on the employee before the employee will act on behalf of the customer. The first law of physics states, "A body at rest tends to remain at rest." Paraphrase this physical law in the workplace and you get, "A work force tends to remain inflexible until acted on by an outside force—lost business." Before you can expect your staff to be flexible, you must demonstrate that being inflexible chases business away.

• *Fear of being chewed out by higher-ups.* This is perhaps the single greatest impediment to an employee making a potentially customer-saving decision. "What will my boss say if I don't consult with her?"

A telephone company manager was asked to fill in for a day as a customer service supervisor. Upon returning from lunch, she was practically tackled by a customer service representative who said, "It's you! I've been looking all over for you because I think I just made a mistake. A customer called and insisted that I give her a seven-cent credit on a call, and I tried to find you and couldn't so I went ahead and gave her the credit. I hope I didn't mess up."

The temporary supervisor later explained what happened to the full-time supervisor. "That's absolutely ridiculous," said the full-time supervisor. "That rep knows she can issue credits without consulting me."

Chances are the customer service representative once issued a credit without consulting a supervisor and had been lambasted. It only takes one chewing out to help an employee learn the difference between what is said and what is done.

As a supervisor, would you feel comfortable with self-service decision making? Would you respond to a poor decision with, "Why on earth did you do that?" or, "Congratulations! You took the initiative to solve the customer's problem"?

Empowerment is just a fancy word until you convince your employees it's not career threatening to make decisions and mistakes.

• *Customers are not trusted.* Employees tend to forget routine customer contact but retain vivid memories of those customers who abuse a company and its policies. The result is a distorted view of how many customers can be trusted. Don't penalize your current customer because some other customer took advantage of your business. There is absolutely no connection between the two individuals.

• *Fear of lost revenue.* As you embark on the journey of empowerment, be prepared for your staff to be tighter with the company's money than you ever imagined. There are two ways for a company to give up money:

1. Offering credits and refunds to dissatisfied customers.
2. Losing customers permanently due to inflexible service.

The reason staff is so hesitant to part with the company's money in credits and refunds is that they can *see* the money lost. They *can't* see the money lost from disappearing customers. It takes a quick mathematics lesson to expose this second and larger form of lost revenue.

Let's say you're a customer of a cable television company. You called to report that your cable wasn't working for a few days and you ask for a couple of days' credit.

"Did you report the outage to us?" the cable representative asks. "No," you say. "Well, in that case I can't give you any credit."

Maybe you don't feel trusted. Maybe it's just the motivation you need to climb up on your roof, reinstall your television antenna, and call the cable company to announce you're a *former* customer.

Let's assume you were paying $30 a month for your cable service. You were asking for a $2 credit on your bill. The customer service representative could see the $2 flying out the door, so she said no. But she had forgotten to multiply. In a single year, the cable company will lose $360 in revenue over a $2 credit. In five years, $1800 will be lost.

Use a similar example with your people. Assign an annual and lifetime dollar value on a customer's business. Show how this amount overshadows the cost of a single credit. It's the fastest way to make what were invisible dollars very easy to see.

What's in It for Me?

Once the major objections have been met, present these benefits:

- *Your job becomes more interesting and rewarding.* The work becomes less routine and more dynamic. You'll be asked to think, not just do.
- *You take personal ownership of the business.* You're transformed from decision giver to decision maker.
- *You'll spend less time searching for your supervisor.* The job gets done more quickly because the power is in your hands, not in your supervisor's.
- *Your customers become more loyal.* The customer who is trusted and accommodated comes back for more. We are attracted to those who show an interest in serving us well.

Next, decide to what extent you want your staff to be empowered. Some businesses are tentative and place a specific dollar limit on employees' credit-issuing power. The limit serves as a safeguard against a frontline employee overstepping the boundaries of common sense. Once the customer request exceeds that limit, the employee is instructed to receive authority from a supervisor.

A better strategy is to offer employees limitless power to satisfy customers. This communicates a sense of trust in the employee's judgment and increases the individual's job satisfaction.

At the Etonic Golf Shoe Division of Etonic Tretorn Puma, customer service representatives are empowered to do what it takes to retain a customer's loyalty. If a customer calls and expresses dissatisfaction with the shoes he's purchased, the customer service representative can offer any new pair of shoes as a replacement—without leaving the telephone.

The Newton, Massachusetts, Marriott Hotel initiated an empowerment program and decided that *all* employees would have the same unlimited power to meet customers' requests and solve customers' problems. The housekeeper's instructions are the same as the general manager's. Do what *you* think will keep the customer satisfied.

The Erin Company, franchisee of seven Holiday Inns, has used both the limited and unlimited method of empowerment. Not only has unlimited power increased customer satisfaction, it has saved the company money.

In their Waterville, Maine, hotel, all the guesswork was removed from resolving customer complaints. If upon check-out, you complained that your television hadn't worked properly, $5 would be automatically credited to your bill. You didn't have to ask. Just call the problem to the hotel's attention and the credit was yours.

Management then thought, "What would happen if we liberated employees from these fixed dollar amounts and asked them to make their own decisions?" The results were immediate and profitable. Employees were free to share decision-making power with their customers. Dissatisfied customers were asked, *"How can we resolve this to your total satisfaction?"*

Some customers with broken televisions didn't feel a credit was necessary. They were satisfied just to know the problem would be corrected for the next guest. It's a win-win situation. The hotel is better satisfying customers while spending less money on credits.[1]

This unlimited power to satisfy:

• Speeds service.
• Increases repeat business.
• Develops employee self-confidence.

Total empowerment also increases the chances that some poor decisions will be made. Most often, a frontline employee will be too stingy. On rare occasions, the employee might behave like my seven-year-old son, Kevin. I was rehearsing a situation with him in which a customer in a restaurant had received a bad bowl of soup. Almost rhetorically, I turned to him and asked, "What should be done for this customer?" "Give her the restaurant," was his response.

A supervisor is now required to walk a new and equally challenging tightrope. How do I correct my employee's decision without discouraging him from making decisions in the future?

Olof Arnheim, general manager of the Newton Marriott says, "The first step is to celebrate that the associate made the decision on the spot. Second, I would explore with my associate what other possible options were available in the situation. After listing the options, I would ask my associate if a better option was listed."[2] A correction is made without sacrificing the associate's motivation to go out and decide again.

Linda Barry, a customer service manager for Federal Express in New Jersey, emphasizes the importance of preparation and coaching. Each representative is trained to handle the most common special requests before the requests occur. The representative is therefore less likely to be surprised or feel ambushed.

Coaching is first asking, "How do you think that call went?" Then she asks, "How else could this call have been handled?" She next would ask, "Do you think any of these alternatives is better than the one you chose?"[3]

Ms. Barry's goal is to help her employee *discover* a better alternative versus delivering what she considers to be the right way. If you say, "You should have done it *this* way," you're inviting your staff to behave as they did in preempowerment times. "I'll have to talk to my boss," will once again echo through your hallways.

A Decision-Making Checklist

Here are the questions each employee should ask himself before making a decision:

• *How likely am I to face this situation again?* If the circumstances are highly unusual and unlikely to be repeated, the employee should lean toward yes. If this is not a precedent-setting event, use that three-letter word that brings your customer back.

• *Would I say yes if it happened again?* If you are setting a precedent, be prepared to offer the same solution to the next customer who presents you with the same situation. A business of integrity will provide the same response to all customers. Being selectively flexible is a ticking time bomb. Assume that customers talk to one another. It's only a matter of time before one customer tells another how a situation was handled and rightfully calls your bluff.

• *Is it fair?* Is it fair not just to the customer but to your business? Is the customer absconding with enough revenue to affect your ability to be profitable? This approach is the most logically effective yet the most underutilized method of explaining why the answer is no. Virtually all customers will be fair but you must first appeal to their sense of fairness.

• *Will my company lose or gain in the long run if I say yes?* Think again of the cable company unwilling to part with $2 but losing hundreds of dollars in the process. The secret is to weigh what is lost short term with the potential gain in the long term.

• *Can I say no in a way that the customer will understand?* Asking this question disciplines you to always offer a "here's why." It also impels you to continually question the need to say no. If you can't explain why, go to someone who can explain the policy. If no one can explain or justify the policy, it's time for the policy to be eliminated.

• *Will my no say, "I don't trust you?"* Questioning a customer's version of events is a black hole. It only makes sense if you have strong cause to doubt the veracity of your customer's story and are willing to risk losing this customer's business. It's hard to imagine that a customer who's lying will suddenly make a dramatic confession under your intensive cross-examination.

Any Special Requests?

Once unleashed, empowerment can cause customers to receive responses as unique as the personality of the employee making the decision. Make an identical request to three different employees and you might receive three different responses.

Each employee should make a note of any new or unusual customer requests. When the department meets, they can be discussed and evaluated using the decision-making checklist. There are three advantages to making this process part of your regular staff meeting:

• Each empowered employee benefits from brainstorming. Many heads are better than one. Either the past decision will be validated by the group or a creative discussion will assure a better decision is made the next time.

• This consensus building increases the chance that a customer receives a common response regardless of which employee makes the decision. Every member of your staff is now "reading off the same page."

• Special requests are frequently the seeds from which excellent new products or services grow.

Full staff meetings are not practical for large, around-the-clock operations. Lands' End, the Dodgeville, Wisconsin, purveyor of mail-order clothing, uses electronic mail (E-mail) to accomplish the same goal. Any representative at any time can post a special situation on E-mail and ask her fellow representatives for suggestions on how to best deal with the customer's request. All customer service representatives freely share their experience and useful information on this electronic bulletin board.

Going to Your Supervisor

Empowerment does not eliminate the need for consulting with supervisors. An effective supervisor will instruct staff members to come to her for policy clarification and explanation, but not constant verification. If an employee is constantly approaching a supervisor and asking, "What do you think I should do?" the best strategy for the supervisor is to ricochet the question and ask the employee, "What do *you* think you should do?" Otherwise, empowerment unravels and the supervisor reprises her role as ultimate and exclusive decision maker.

If you tell your customer you are going to check with your supervisor, *put the customer on hold.* Push the hold button on your telephone. A customer should not be straining to listen to what's being said and decided.

This means *getting out of the view* of the customer if the contact is face-to-face. Few things are more frustrating to customers than making a special request and then watching a two-person huddle across the room. The customer's imagination and frustration run wild. "What are they saying about me? Why can't that supervisor just walk over here and talk to me?"

Frontline Yes/Supervisor No

When a frontline employee and a supervisor share the decision-making process, any good news should be delivered by the frontline employee. If the supervisor is the one delivering the good news, customers are led to believe that the only way to receive a yes is to ask for a supervisor.

It's equally important that the *supervisor* deliver bad news. Consider the following scenario: A customer makes a special request to a frontline employee. The frontline employee, unsure of how to respond, checks with the supervisor. The customer waits while the frontline employee and the supervisor form a decision-making huddle. The two employees break up the huddle but only the frontline employee returns to the line of scrimmage.

When the answer is no, the customer's frustration level enters the stratosphere. "What was the supervisor's reason? Why am I forced to hear this decision interpreted by a frontline employee rather than hearing it directly from the person who made it?" The customer's next request is justified and predictable: "I want to talk to your supervisor."

Saving Face

Suppose a customer makes a special request to an empowered frontline employee. The employee uses the decision-making checklist, decides to say "No, here's why, but here's what I can do . . ." This response is not good enough for this rather inflexible and demanding customer. The customer's response is, "I want to talk to your supervisor."

Let's say *you* are that supervisor. Your frontline employee made the right decision. Yet to defend that decision risks losing this customer. What's the right thing to do?

What happens too often is that the supervisor reverses the decision, the customer walks away happy, and the frontline employee feels like crawling in a hole. There is a better way:

1. Decide whether you want to back up your frontline employee's decision. Maybe it *was* the right call.

2. Whether you do or do not change the decision, tell the customer that the frontline employee handled the request in exactly the correct manner.
3. If you decide to offer a different response, explain *why* your response is different from the one just communicated by the frontline employee.
4. Tell your frontline employee what was said to the customer—that the situation was handled correctly. Then share the reasons you reached a different decision than he did. You may also let him know that the next time he faces a similar situation, he is empowered to make the same exception you just made.

Nothing destroys morale in an organization more completely than telling employees to make decisions and then simply reversing those decisions. Nothing strengthens a sense of teamwork like fully supporting each employee's sometimes risky effort to learn and grow.

Employees will also strive to treat all customers the same, whether they provide $10 million or $10 worth of business. A mixed message is received by an employee who's told that an exception was made this time, "because she's a good customer." Such logic infers that some customers are better than others. Employees don't want to fawn over big wheels or grease only squeaky wheels. They want *all* wheels treated the same.

When you support your employee's growth and treat your customers fairly, your people will bend over backwards to help you succeed.

Here are the three ideas from this chapter that I will use right away:

1. _____

2. _____

3. _____

Chapter Four

Irate Customers

It began so innocently. Mary set her alarm and drifted off to sleep. Rrrrrrrrring!!!!!! She grapples for the phone. "Hello," she mumbles. "Hi, I'd like to order a large pepperoni and a medium sausage and peppers." This is the third pizza call Mary's received this week. "When I get up tomorrow," she says, "I'm calling the phone company to change my number." She spends several restless hours thinking about all of her possible new phone numbers. Before she knows it, her daughter is tugging at her blanket.

"Mommy, I have a stomach ache." Her daughter hops into bed. Moments later, the alarm sounds. "I don't want to go to school," her daughter pleads. Mary suspects that this sudden ailment has been conveniently timed. A bargaining session begins.

"What if I were to drive you to school?" Mary says. Suddenly, Mary's daughter feels better. If only the same could be said for Mary's car. It won't start. Mary's daughter is now late for school, which means . . . guess who else is late?

Mary arrives at her desk and finds a "please see me" note on the top of her telephone. It's from her supervisor. "What did I do wrong now?" she thinks. Her supervisor's office door is closed. She decides to come back later. Mary returns to her desk ready to take her first call from a customer. But what's she *really* ready for?

Trouble. If a customer calls who's had the same kind of morning Mary has, we may witness a company's worst nightmare—the irate customer meets the irate employee. When an employee responds to anger with anger, there are serious consequences:

1. The irate customer becomes a former customer.
2. The irate employee who loses his/her cool creates a personal memory that lasts a lifetime.

WHY IS MARY SO VULNERABLE?

Blame it on her ancestors. To fully understand why people sometimes "lose their cool," we should visit one of Mary's ancient relatives, the caveman. There he is, hundreds of thousands of years ago, sitting in his cave. He didn't have car problems or receive "please see me" notes, but he faced his own set of stressors. Imagine he walks out of his cave ready for a successful day of hunting only to find a wild tiger has decided to save him the trip.

Instantly, the danger is recognized. His eyes receive the image. His brain tells his endocrine system to begin secreting a form of adrenalin called epinephrine. This hormone causes the sugar stored in his liver to be released into the blood stream. It also triggers the heart to begin pumping furiously and the lungs to operate more efficiently, sending large quantities of blood to his muscles. His hands, feet, and digestive organs receive less blood flow. The body sets its priorities. Digesting breakfast is last on the list.

Increased blood flow to his brain helps him make the most important decision of his life: Do I stay and engage in "hand to paw" combat or do I attempt to set a world record in the five-mile run? His body is now prepared for either choice. The Herculean strength and endurance needed to survive this encounter have been assured. His arms and legs are filled with the oxygenated blood and energy needed to do battle or to endure the fastest, longest run of his life.

Upon completion of the battle or run, the caveman is totally exhausted and drops off for hours of restorative sleep.

We should be grateful for the ground-breaking research of Dr. Walter B. Cannon in the early 1900s. He helped us gain a better understanding of how the human body responds to physical danger. He was the first person to identify the *fight/flight response* and described it as a hormonal reaction, "common to man and beast," as a reflex, "not a willed movement."[1]

Here are the steps in the fight/flight response:

1. Danger recognized.
2. Energy created.
3. Energy expended.
4. Rest and restoration to normal hormonal/body function.

We should be similarly grateful that the fight/flight response is ready to serve us today and tomorrow should we encounter a wild tiger or any other threat to our physical survival. It is an *involuntary* response in the face of physical danger. Unfortunately, the fight/flight response can be triggered by *emotional* threats as well. In this case, the response is chosen, or *voluntary*. What choice will Mary make?

If her first customer of the day proceeds to tell her that she is ignorant and that she is personally responsible for every problem he has ever had in doing business with her company, and if he includes in his monologue several words Mary hasn't heard since she was in the navy, Mary's . . .

- Adrenal glands begin to secrete epinephrine.
- Heart rate doubles.
- Blood sugar becomes elevated.
- Blood pressure soars.

If she doesn't take some steps to arrest these physical changes, Mary will find herself confounding the evolutionary process and behaving exactly like her ancient ancestor. In this encounter, the customer has an unfair advantage. He can behave in any way he chooses. Mary cannot. He can use abusive language. Mary cannot. He can both create *and* expend the energy of a threatened caveman. Mary is permitted only the first half of the process—she can *create* the energy, but to *expend* the energy is to risk losing both a customer and a job.

WHAT'S A PROFESSIONAL CUSTOMER CONTACT PERSON TO DO?

First, recognize that all human beings are subject to the stressors Mary faced last night and early this morning. The chances are excellent that Mary's customer is behaving like a caveman because he didn't sleep last night and his kids were sick and his car wouldn't start. The stressors of the day are not reserved for those who work with customers. Sometimes your customer's having as rough a time as you are.

Second, *frustrations are cumulative*. One stressor doesn't take the place of another. It is thrown on the pile. Let's say you wake up late and then discover your car won't start. The car not starting doesn't *replace* the stress of oversleeping; it adds to it.

One Piece of Straw

In arid parts of the globe, camels have been used for centuries as work animals, transporting food and supplies over great distances. Every camel has a maximum load it can endure. Exceed that load factor and the camel's back can literally be broken. The same is true for us. When we face personal hardships, our emotional load becomes heavy. We may even strain at the breaking point. One more phone call, one more piece of bad news and we may "break," behaving in ways that would be unthinkable under better circumstances.

For customers, a delinquency notice, a defective part, a promise broken can be the "straw that broke the camel's back" or "the *last* straw." Remember that you or your business are only a single straw from a heavy load, yet if you are the last straw, your customer will unload the entire pile on you. Why is this important? Because you should remember that you are rarely the root *cause* of the customer's anger, only the recipient of it.

Third, *frustrations are transferrable.* As much as we'd like to live in separately sealed emotional compartments—home life and work life—we tend to take our stressors with us on our daily commute. The beginning of our day at home affects our behavior at work. Have a smooth start to the day, and the most difficult customer becomes a challenge rather than a threat. But if you wake up late, run out of clean clothes, miss breakfast, and get stuck in traffic, the angry customer is no longer a challenge but someone who should be taught a lesson. You find yourself rehearsing what you would say if you really didn't need your job.

You might face all of these stressors in the morning. You might bring them to work and still you are expected to be a pleasant person. Your employer is asking you on these days to "manufacture" pleasantness, to act pleasant, even if you don't feel it. Sociologist Arlie Hochschild describes this as "emotional labor."[2] You're being asked to act in a way you don't genuinely feel.

This acting is a necessity. Sometimes genuine pleasantness isn't possible and it becomes necessary to create it. With most customers the emotional investment pays immediate dividends. Customers often respond to pleasantness with pleasantness. When you receive pleasantness, your need to "act" is diminished. As your contact with customers progresses, you find yourself feeling more pleasant and less dependent on the act.

This will be true for most, but not all, customers. Some customers call you or approach you with their own pile of stressors near the breaking point. If this customer engages in "caveman behavior," your act begins to unravel and you run the risk of responding in kind. Add these additional stressors and you become even more vulnerable to the fight/flight response:

1. *Fatigue:* When you are tired, your body's "trigger point" is narrowed.
2. *Hunger:* Often overlooked as a factor. Low blood sugar prompts a correspondingly higher level of epinephrine. You're more likely to behave like a caveman on an empty stomach.
3. *Caffeine:* Creates some of the same bodily changes as epinephrine. Your pulse rate and blood sugar are temporarily increased.
4. *Heat:* Remember the last time you were in a traffic jam on a 90-degree day? Surrounded by people testing their horns, weren't you? Nothing shortens a person's fuse like record high temperatures.

Think of these factors as ingredients in a very dangerous recipe. Stir them together and you'll find yourself doing an excellent impersonation of one of *your* ancient ancestors.

PREVENTING THE CAVEMAN RESPONSE

Use this four-step method to deal with irate customers:

1. *Let 'em rip.* Give your customer the chance to expend the energy created by the fight/flight response. Like the caveman, once the energy is expended, the customer becomes fatigued and loses his/her desire to fight. The customer should be allowed to speak, yell, or scream without correction or interruption. Much of what you'll hear at this stage will be inaccurate or untrue. Accept it. There will be opportunities to set the record straight later in the conversation. It's also important that you engage in what we'll call selective listening. This is the process of *hearing* all of what the customer says but only *listening* for those comments that help you solve the customer's problem.

There is good reason for this. It's during this "let 'em rip" stage that a customer may bait you with tempting comments or remarks. They'll be dangled in front of you with the hope you'll bite. Once you raise your voice, interrupt, or in any other way lose your cool, you're on the hook and the customer has slipped off. "What's so wrong with me yelling at him?" the customer now silently says. "Listen to the way he's speaking to me!"

Several years ago, I sat with a new customer service representative (CSR) and listened to him handle a few calls. It wasn't long before he was dealing with a real live VIP (Very Irate Person). During the call, the customer turned slightly away from the phone to someone in her apartment and said, "Oh, this guy must be new down there. He doesn't know what he's doing."

How would *you* respond to such a comment? Without missing a beat, the CSR said, "Ma'am, I'm *not* new down here, and I *do* know what I'm doing."

The customer had suddenly brought the CSR off the higher level he had occupied and onto her level. In the months that followed, that CSR surely learned to let such customers' comments "pass through." Responding brought him no closer to solving the customer's problem.

Selective listening becomes easier when you hold the phone or the headset slightly away from your ear. Loosen your grip on the phone. The tighter the grip, the greater the chance that your adrenalin will begin to flow. If you're face to face with the customer, take a slow step backward. The closer you are to the customer, the greater the chance your pulse rate will soar.

If the customer is "letting it rip" in a public place, offer to take him or her to a less disruptive location, perhaps a nearby office. You might say something like this: "Let's see if we can find a place where I can give you my full and undivided attention."

Listen for words that are clues to the true source of the customer's anger. Say just enough to let the customer know that you're listening. When you feel that you have a good handle on the customer's situation and sense that the customer has fully expended the energy, say something like, "Is there anything else I should know?" When the answer you receive is no, move to step two.

2. *Report what you've heard to the customer.* Have you noticed how some people can watch a two-hour movie and neatly summarize it for you in less than a minute? This is the skill you can use with your angry customer. Start with, "Let me make sure I understand what you've said." Then begin your summation. It proves you've listened. It gives the customer the chance to say, "No, that's not why I'm upset." You may not get it right every time, but even the angriest customer will appreciate that you're making the effort. Most of all, the customer wants to feel understood. Keep

trying until the customer tells you that you have understood. Now move to step three:

3. *Ask the customer to solve the problem.* This is the turning point in many encounters with VIPs. It's unexpected. You've hit the ball into the customer's court and said, "Hit back any shot you want." You're forcing your customer to think and a customer can't think and be angry at the same time.

The customer often has a better solution than you do. The customer has been thinking about this situation—sometimes for days. By contrast, you've been ambushed by the customer's call or visit. You put unnecessary pressure on yourself when you expect to create instant solutions to customer's problems. Let the customer go first.

The other unexpected benefit of asking the customer for a solution is that the customer often suggests a solution less expensive than the solution you were about to offer. Your company saves money, and nothing makes a customer happier than her own solution to a problem.

Once you've heard the customer's solution, determine whether it can be immediately accepted. Should you have any doubts, offer to think it over or to speak with some others at your company. This allows both you and your customer a "cooling off" period. It also proves you're giving serious consideration to what the customer has proposed.

To ask the customer for a solution and then to immediately say, "I can't do that," is to leave the customer thinking, "Why did he ask in the first place?" If you've been assured that your company cannot live with the customer's solution, move to step four:

4. *Make a counter-offer.* You are now negotiating with the hope you'll propose a solution that satisfies both your company and your customer. "Here's what I can do" sounds much better to a customer than, "I can't do that." Continue the back and forth of this process, negotiating a solution in good faith.

This four-step method will work in most cases. It assumes that your day hasn't included heat, hunger, excess caffeine, and fatigue.

Perhaps you're having a day like our friend Mary—or worse. If someone in your family is seriously ill, or you're facing a sudden financial crisis, you may find yourself stuck at that first step—the "let 'em rip" stage, unable to use the skills outlined above.

I hope you've made some friends in your workplace. This is when you'll need them!

The Buddy System

When you feel your heart pounding and your antiperspirant being tested, consider passing the customer along to a co-worker. There are several advantages:

• Your co-worker hasn't been listening to what you have. He/she enters the call in a much calmer state of mind than your present one.

• The irate customer tends to behave like a caveman with you and a decent human being with your buddy. Most irate customers have a fixed amount of accumulated frustrations that they'll unload on you. Given this chance to "let it rip," most will calm down. By the time your customer reaches your buddy, he/she's ready to discuss solutions.

• The customer feels a sense of progress. "I must be speaking to someone in a position of authority." It is not necessary that the buddy be a manager or a supervisor.

What *is* necessary is that what gets passed along with the call is all the information your buddy will need to effectively assist the customer. *A customer should not have to repeat his/her story to your buddy.* Forcing a customer to do so is inviting him/her to become irate all over again.

This is not to suggest that you pick the one person in your workplace you don't like and pass all your VIPs to that one individual. This is a responsibility to be equally shared. Be prepared to return the favor upon request.

Prolonged Profanity

It may have surprised you on your first day of work that some customers' remarks would be unprintable in any respectable newspaper. A reporter might write that your customer's favorite word is "expletive." Am I expected to tolerate such language? Shouldn't I just hang up on such behavior? I don't get paid to listen to this, do I?

You should accept this language during the initial "let 'em rip" stage of the conversation. Many customers approach you with a full load of frustrations. The load becomes unbearable and the breaking point is reached.

Suddenly, an otherwise reasonable person finds himself using language normally reserved for locker rooms and bad drivers. In fact, some customers are so enraged that they don't even realize they're using profanity.

There is a limit to what a customer service professional should accept. If there seems to be no end to the profanity, there are several possible strategies:

• *Use the buddy system.* The customer's language and temperament may improve when speaking to the buddy.

• *Offer a fair professional warning.* The goal is to call attention to the language while affording the customer the chance to change his/her behavior. You should also explain that unless the language changes, the call will come to an end: "Mr. Brown, I'm here to help you. But I'm afraid if you continue to use that kind of language, I'll have to end the conversation."

A customer service representative in Ohio suggests this version: "Mrs. Gray, I'm here to help you. But if we can't continue this call in a business-like manner, I'll have to end the call." If the customer continues to use profanity, you would then disconnect the call. It's important that employees have this safety valve. To insist that the employee stay on the phone under any and all circumstances is to subject that employee to undue and unfair stress. Sometimes the choice is between staying on the line and losing your cool or avoiding the risk by ending the call.

If this warning is well presented, if your words are carefully chosen, the customer's language will change. *Do not expect to improvise this warning.* Many customer contact professionals have a typewritten copy of these warnings directly above their telephones so they can read off the page when necessary.

The fair professional warning should be a last resort. It's better to use the buddy system if a buddy is available. Accept as much profanity as you can. Only when you hear your ancient ancestor knocking on your door should you read your lines. Veteran customer service representatives report that in entire careers the need to disconnect a customer has occurred only a handful of times.

If you find that a member of your staff is prematurely ending calls on a regular basis, the chances are that the problem rests not with the temperament of your customers, but with that of your employee.

Anne-Marie's idea. Anne-Marie Eugley, of North Shore Medical Center (Salem, Mass.), avoids the fair professional warning by using a totally different approach:

"Mr. Jones, I just want you to know you can say anything you want in this conversation, and I'm not going to hang up."[3]

Notice that Anne-Marie has called attention to Mr. Jones' language but without even a hint of confrontation. She reports that not only does Mr. Jones clean up his language, but he usually apologizes for it as well.

Anne-Marie's method is the preferred method. But it only works when you mean what you say. Are you willing to accept anything the customer says? If not, the words will sound hollow to you and the customer.

Face-to-face contact. What if you work at a register or a service counter? How should you deal with profane language? When possible, ask a co-worker or supervisor to wait on the customer.

What if you're face to face with a profane customer and there is no buddy available? This is one of the most challenging situations in customer service.

• *Make eye contact.* Show your willingness to listen and to accept the customer's anger.

• *Say as little as possible.* The customer experiencing the fight/flight response has jumped off a psychological cliff and wants to use you as a parachute. As soon as you respond to one of the customer's baiting remarks, he feels some justification for his behavior.

• *Talk to yourself.* This is the moment when you must remind yourself, "This person will not be in front of me for the rest of my life. The less I say, the sooner she'll leave." This self-talk is necessary because, at that moment, it feels as if the customer *will* be in front of you for the rest of your life.

The Customer's Gone but My Heart's Still Pounding!

• *Take a break.* This is when you are most vulnerable. Dealing with back-to-back irate customers is a sure way to become an irate employee. Stand up. Walk away from your work space. Visit the water cooler. Take two very large deep breaths.

In an insurance office in New Hampshire, new customer service representatives are taught to head for the door on the far wall that opens directly outside. They then stick their faces out and breathe in the weather of the day. As you might imagine, this technique is especially effective in January.

• *Walk at lunch.* Louise spent over 30 years working as a customer service representative for a golf company in Massachusetts. She rarely missed her noontime walk, explaining that she always returned to work in a better frame of mind. Countless people have attested to the effectiveness of this 15-minute recess in a stressful day.

But There's This Good Listener Who Sits Next to Me . . .

This is an easy but totally ineffective way to release the energy created from dealing with an irate customer. In her book *Anger—The Misunderstood Emotion*, Carol Tavris shatters the myth that talking out anger gets rid of it. Instead, the talker relives it.[4]

Imagine the talker having a wheelbarrow filled with frustrations, approaching the listener fully expecting that if the wheelbarrow is tipped forward, it will empty. Just the opposite occurs. The wheelbarrow is *reloaded.*

Think of a time when a friend told you of a bad encounter with a person or business. If you watched carefully, you could almost see your friend's blood pressure and pulse rate rise. It is better to walk it off than to talk it off.

TIPS FROM THE PROS

Here are real world, tested ideas to prevent "losing it."

• *Put yourself on hold.* It is not the customer who's put on hold, it is your emotions. Under less stressful circumstances, you might ask permission to put the customer on hold. If you feel you're about to lose it, "I'm going to put you on hold for a moment" is sufficient.

• *Walk away.* Physically remove yourself from the place of confrontation. Those who perform in-home service work occasionally walk to their trucks in order to gain a minute's respite from an angry customer.

• *Breathe deeply.* A few slow deep breaths will actually counteract the tendency for the fight/flight response.

• *Take a mental vacation.* This is an Alcoholics Anonymous idea. A recovering alcoholic is taught to relieve stress by closing her eyes and picturing herself in a place she finds totally calm and serene. Everyone has his/her own mental vacation spot. Here's the best way to discover yours. Once you've read this paragraph, close your eyes, take a deep breath, and picture in your mind's eye a place that makes you feel totally relaxed and at peace. Hold that image for at least 10 seconds. The next time you're in a high-stress situation, take a 10-second mental vacation to the place you just imagined.

• *Picture for perspective.* Place a snapshot in your work area of one or more of the most important people in your life. While you're on hold, look down at that picture and remember who you really work for. Some people prefer to use a snapshot of a favorite pet. The ideal would be a snapshot of your favorite people at your favorite place.

It's possible to combine some of these ideas from the pros. A service technician in Virginia has a picture of his wife and two children on the dashboard of his truck. If he's in the home of a VIP, he'll excuse himself, walk to the truck and say to himself, "I work for them (looking at the picture), not for them (the name on the work order)." The matter placed in perspective, he returns to the house ready to meet the customer's needs.

A customer service representative for a major software company added her own wrinkle to this perspective idea. One day, she returned from lunch to find a voice mail message from her husband. She smiled as she listened: "Hi honey. I just called to tell you that you're the most important person in my life and I love you very much."

She saved the message—not for the day, but for good. Whenever a VIP calls her, she'll say, "I'm going to put you on hold for just a moment." You can probably guess what happens next. She retrieves her voice mail message and hears: "Hi honey. I just called to tell you that you're the most important person in my life and I love you very much."

• *Drop your pen.* This may be your only way to put a face-to-face customer on hold. Nudge your pen to the edge of the counter and let it fall. Excuse yourself and take your time retrieving it, breathing deeply as you do. Don't forget to come back up!

• *Compliment the customer's anger.* This may sound unrealistic but many customer contact people report using it with success: "Mr. Delacruz, you're handling this situation much better than I would. If this happened to me, I'd be much more upset than you are."

What Not *to Do*

• *Describing the customer's behavior to the customer.* You might be tempted to say, "You seem to be quite angry about this." Or, "You're sounding quite hostile at the moment." A customer does not want to be reminded that he is angry. Your job is to provide service, not psychotherapy.

• *Using humor.* A customer in the middle of a full blown fight/flight outburst has no sense of humor. Some employees claim to have the ability to diffuse anger by helping a customer to see the funny side of the situation. In most cases, you'll only stoke the flames.

TURN IT OFF OR BURN IT OFF

The caveman experiencing the fight/flight response had a fundamental advantage over men and women of our era. He created *and* expended the energy.

Dr. Cannon provided us with this health warning back in 1911: "If these results of emotions and pain are not 'worked off' by action, it is conceivable that the excessive adrenin and sugar may have pathological effects."[5]

There are two tools at your disposal to prevent or dispose of these effects— your mind and your body.

Dr. Herbert Benson, an associate professor of Medicine at Harvard Medical School, has built on Dr. Cannon's research and discovered that a person can mentally short circuit the fight/flight response, thus blocking the body's tendency to secrete epinephrine and to dump sugar into the bloodstream. He calls it the relaxation response.[6]

To practice the relaxation response, you choose a focus word or a short phrase that's rooted in your personal belief system. You then sit quietly, close your eyes, relax your muscles, and breathe slowly and naturally, repeating your focus word or phrase as you exhale. Benson points out that it's important to assume a passive attitude, not worrying about how well you're doing. Continue the process for 10 to 20 minutes and practice it once or twice a day for maximum results.[7]

Clinical studies have shown this technique can shut down the fight/flight response. Though Dr. Benson concedes that this entire process is not practical while facing an angry customer, you can use parts of the process—the focus word, the breathing techniques—to inhibit an angry response. He also argues that the person who practices the relaxation response *before* work is more likely to control his emotions *during* work.[8]

The other method is the old fashioned way—burning it off physically. The caveman could swing his club. You can use a much more civilized method through aerobic exercise. Exercise provides you a safe and productive way to use up the energy accumulated in a day of dealing with irate customers. You expend the energy of a caveman without behaving like one.

AVOIDING THE BOILING POINT

Many customers contact your company because something has gone wrong. They're not calling intent on being difficult. What's most important to them is that the problem be fixed. They arrive on the edge of irateness. You'll be given a chance to solve the problem, but use any of the following expressions and you'll send them over the edge:

• *"I can't do that. It's against company policy."* This is an insufficient and unsatisfactory response to any customer request. Entrepreneur Paul Hawken points out that the word *policy* has as its root the word *police*. Are you here to meet customer needs or to enforce the law? Explain *why* you can't do it. Company policy is a smoke screen often used to avoid making tough decisions.

• *"You're wrong."* Time and again you've heard that the customer is always right. But what about the customer you suspect or know is lying? You may not believe that the customer is always right but the customer should never be told that she is wrong. Dealing with the most difficult customers can be boiled down to this: The difference between a professional and an amateur is that a professional has a seven-second delay between what he's thinking and what comes out of his mouth. An amateur thinks and speaks simultaneously.

• *"But the computer says . . ."* Your customer doesn't care what the computer says. It may not be accurate. It's better to say, "Let me tell you what I see when I pull up your account."

• *"You'll have to talk to . . ."* This opening line can bring out the Mt. Vesuvius in even the most mellow customer. When a customer explains his problem to you and you determine that you are not the person or department who can solve his problem you should:

1. Transfer him to the person in your company who can solve the problem.
2. Explain to this problem solver as much as the customer has explained to you.

A customer should only have to make one call to your company to resolve a problem. A customer should only have to tell his story once. *Take ownership for the customer's problem until the customer owns a solution.*

THE ATTITUDE OF ANTICIPATION

The employee who *expects* to deal with angry people deals with plenty of angry people. By contrast, the employee who enjoys working with people rarely encounters a customer who can't be appeased. Your attitude of anticipation determines your caseload of problem customers. If the customer walks up to you or the phone rings and you say to yourself, "I bet you this one's going to be a winner," guess what? You've predicted the near future with surprising accuracy. Customers can feel your attitude, even over the phone. Tom Peters and Nancy Austin call this Thinly Disguised Contempt or TDC.[9]

Some employees display TDC by using the thermometer approach. Their response to a customer is solely dependent on the behavior of the customer. The reasoning goes something like this: "Be nice to me, I'll be nice to you. Be nasty to me and I'll return your nastiness." The customer's temperature is measured and reflected. Inherent in this attitude is, "Let the customer go first. I'll react."

The professional's approach is, "*I'll* go first by being pleasant and let the customer respond." It is the willingness to use emotional labor. It's the opposite of TDC—it's ACR—Assuming the Customer is Reasonable. When you do, most customers will be.

When you anticipate meeting the needs of even the most difficult customers, you stack the odds in your favor. Ninety-eight percent of your customers are reasonable people who will only behave unreasonably under strain or provocation. This figure is not based on scientific data, but on experience.

Ninety-eight percent of your angry customers are not a problem, but an opportunity. They tell you how to improve your business in ways satisfied customers never do. When you keep your cool—when you transform your customers from irateful to grateful—your business grows as we'll see in the next chapter.

Here are the three ideas from this chapter that I will use right away:

1. _____

2. _____

3. _____

Chapter Five

The Art of Recovery

Suppose you eat in a restaurant for the first time. Your main course arrives, a fish dish that smells like the fish has been loitering at the restaurant for days. The waiter approaches and asks, "How is everything?"

Because you've never had assertiveness training, you respond, "Fine." What the waiter does next will determine whether you ever visit this restaurant again. If he accepts your one-word response, you'll walk out the door and never return. If *he's* had assertiveness training, he may go a step further saying, "Are you sure it's fine? You don't seem to be enjoying it." Now convinced that the waiter is genuinely interested in your satisfaction, you speak up. Thus begins the process of *recovery*.

Recovery is transforming a dissatisfied customer into a satisfied one. It has two critical parts:

- Capturing customer dissatisfaction.
- Correcting the mistake to the customer's satisfaction.

You can be highly skilled in both of these areas and still have a failing business. You might offer a money-back guarantee and discover that all of your customers want their money back. While some experts argue that transforming customers from irateful to grateful actually increases customer loyalty, the best strategy is to:

- Produce a product/service of such consistently high quality that the occasions of recovery are practically zero.
- Be prepared for recovery situations. You won't please all the people all of the time.

Legal Sea Foods, Inc., a restaurant chain based in the Boston area, is an excellent example of a business skilled in recovery avoidance. Unlike the restaurant in our opening example, Legal never faces this recovery situation by simply refusing to serve a bad piece of fish. Legal purchases only "top of the catch" right off the boat, meaning the fish you eat tonight was probably in the ocean less than 24 hours ago. And once caught, the poor fish never gets a moment to itself. Eight separate quality inspections are performed during its journey from the boat to your plate. Like all thriving businesses, Legal Sea Foods knows that the best strategy is to deliver a quality product the first time, every time.[1]

You may feel confident that your product is satisfying your customers, but is your intuition enough?

Eliciting customer feedback is critical. Former New York City Mayor Ed Koch had the right idea. Each time he walked the streets of his city, he'd greet his constituents/customers with, "How am I doing?" If you don't ask the question, you won't get an answer.

HOW *DID* WE DO?

How are *you* asking the question? Some large companies hire telephone research firms to call a random sample of customers to determine customer satisfaction. The results of these surveys can be compared over a period of time so that the company can see whether it's providing consistently high-quality service. Dissatisfaction may be captured but usually in an anonymous way. Recovery may be needed but the individual customers who are dissatisfied may not be identified. You'll get an idea of how you're doing but may miss the opportunity to recover. Telephone research should:

• *Make a customer feel important.* A professional researcher will emphasize to the customer being questioned how valuable his input is and describe what the business intends to do with it.

• *Permit and record open-ended responses.* Customers often have more to say than "strongly agree" or "somewhat disagree." Design a survey that provides you with more detailed information.

• *Collect names and phone numbers for follow-up.* A dissatisfied customer's name and phone number should be retrieved and then called by the business. The second phase of the recovery process can then begin.

Comment cards are another popular way of asking the question. But poorly designed comment cards can give you a false sense of security. If you ask questions and provide room for only yes/no responses and offer no lines for customer comments, a dissatisfied customer might assume you aren't really interested in hearing bad news. An effective comment card is:

• *Return postage paid.* Don't expect a dissatisfied customer to pay the freight.

• *Scaled for responses.* The customer should have more than a yes/no option. Ask customers to rate their level of satisfaction as excellent, good, fair, or poor. A numerical scale is also effective. For example, you could ask for ratings on a one-to-five scale with five being the highest rating and one being the lowest.

• *Rated left to right.* The card should be designed so that rating scales move left to right with excellent on the left and poor on the right. This is the most common format. Trying to be different may confuse your respondent.

• *Eye catching.* Many hotel chains place comment cards in their rooms. Sonesta Hotel comment cards are unique. The front panel reads, "WHO CARES?" In small print you see, "We do." If you don't grab your customer's attention, you won't get the feedback.

Posting and Boasting

Many company's comment cards seem designed solely to collect compliments. The company seems to be saying to customers, "Tell us we were wonderful." The company then displays these flattering comments in a public space for all new customers to read and admire. Such businesses fail to realize that a new customer is not interested in how wonderfully other customers were served. The new customer reaches his own conclusion based on how *he* is served.

The best way for your business to get out of the "tell us we were wonderful" trap is to ask a single open-ended question: "Please tell us how we can improve." Provide plenty of writing space and watch what happens. The customer recognizes that his comment card will not be used as waiting room wallpaper but as a tool to build a better business. See the sample comment card on page 74.

Marriott® Hotels • Resorts • Suites—A Case Study

Few businesses relied more heavily on comment cards than Marriott Corporation. They were the hotel's primary measuring stick, evaluating every aspect of a customer's stay. The cards provided the numbers showing

DO YOU HAVE SOMETHING TO TELL US?   *shaw's*

We welcome any suggestion that will help
us to serve you better because **you're
someone special at Shaw's.**

DATE _____

_____
_____
_____
_____
_____
_____
_____
_____
_____
_____
_____
_____
_____
_____

NAME _____

STREET & NO. _____

CITY _____ ZIP _____

Tel. No. _____

which hotel departments best served customers' needs. Each department had goals to meet or beat and competed with other departments for the highest rankings from customers.

The cards were ubiquitous—in lobbies, room dressers, courtesy vans, sometimes even in bathrooms. But it seemed overnight the comment cards disappeared. Why?

Marriott determined this scattershot distribution approach wasn't giving them an accurate measure of customer sentiment. Those most likely to fill out the cards were the very satisfied or the very dissatisfied. The vast majority of customers in between weren't being heard.

Marriott now mails a more comprehensive questionnaire to a randomly selected sample of recent guests. More probing questions are asked and more enlightening responses are received. Using a mailed questionnaire method might decrease the quantity but increase the quality of customer feedback.

The hotel chain also offers an instant feedback tool to all guests during their stay. Next to each guest room phone is a card that urges the customer to dial extension 55 if they have any questions or problems. In most hotels, these calls ring directly to the property's guest relations manager. Other Marriott hotels rotate responsibility for these calls to various managers. Some managers carry a portable phone throughout the day so that guests' calls can be answered directly without the need of a transfer. This allows the hotel to uproot dissatisfaction while the guest is still on the property and to recover immediately.[2]

If you have no feedback system in place, you may want to begin by using customer comment cards. Experts agree that comment cards are not a comprehensive barometer of customer satisfaction but they do provide a quick reading of how well you're doing. It's important to recognize that one dissatisfied customer often speaks for many others and that improvement isn't possible unless someone's telling you how to improve. Too many struggling businesses ask themselves why they're not succeeding when they should be asking their customers.

WHAT *SHOULD* WE DO?

One of the best methods for recovery avoidance is to talk to customers *before* you produce your product or service.

Among the most successful automobile introductions in history was the Ford Taurus®.[†] The late Lewis C. Veraldi, vice president of car product development at Ford, learned the lessons of listening when he oversaw the production of the Ford Fiesta®[†] in Europe. Veraldi brought a completely new way of creating a car to this side of the Atlantic. Every Ford department was expected to participate. Engineering listened to manufacturing; marketing spoke to engineering; even public affairs added their own unique perspective on what the Taurus should be. Team Taurus was born.

But there was one other member added to the team—the customer. Customers were asked the right questions, and Ford developed a car with features that its designers had never considered. For example, have you ever been under the hood of a car and wondered which dipstick was for the motor oil? Plenty of Ford's customers had. They suggested that the oil

---

[†] Registered trademarks of Ford Motor Company.

dipstick be painted yellow to make it easy to find. How about trying to find where to pour in the oil? The oil cap was also painted yellow. Better to ask for input during the design stage than to recover after the product is in the marketplace.[3]

Lotus Development, Microsoft Corporation, and other major computer software manufacturers create test sites, known as beta sites, months before a new product is shipped. Customers are asked to try out new software and report to the manufacturer what they like and don't like. This allows Lotus and the others to fine-tune and correct bugs in the product prior to mass introduction. Customers help them "nip problems in the bud," eliminating the need to recover later.

Mattel, Inc., knows that toy fads come and go. But there's one young lady who never goes out of style—Barbie®. The world's favorite miniaturized teenager is kept forever fresh with a constant new wardrobe and group of accessories. Barbie always *looked* good; Mattel decided it was time to make her *sound* good. Mattel introduced Teen Talk Barbie®. She came complete with an internal microchip that stored four phrases to be spoken at the request of her proud new owner.

Mattel did some homework—but not quite enough. They surveyed children and determined which expressions would be most pleasing to the intended owners. But one of the selected phrases sounded like fingernails scraping on a chalkboard to an unexpected customer—the American Association of University Women. Barbie was taught to say, "Math class is tough." The University Women objected to Mattel, stating that Barbie's lament only perpetuates the stereotype that girls fare poorly in math compared to boys. If Barbie's discouraged with math, why wouldn't her owner begin to feel the same way?

Mattel acquiesced to the protests and Barbie no longer makes discouraging comments about mathematics. Given the chance to do it over again, perhaps her creators would have broadened the definition of a customer. Educators would be asked, "What should we do?" and Mattel would do more listening before Barbie started talking.[4]

Working the Room

The most effective feedback is face-to-face. If you manage a business where customers visit on-site, like a restaurant, a bank, or a supermarket, spend some time each day chatting with people waiting in line and ask people how well you're serving their needs. "What can we do to improve?" "Is there anything you see at our competitors that you prefer to our way of doing business?" Make it clear that you're not just fishing for compliments. If your customers know you're sincere in seeking ways to improve, they'll respond with a sincere effort to help you improve.

Saturday Morning Meetings

Stew Leonard's Dairy of Norwalk, Connecticut, is more than a dairy. It's one of the most successful food stores in the world. They stay successful by listening and reacting to customer requests.

One Saturday a month, a group of customers is invited to sit down with some of the store's managers and share what they like and what they don't like about doing business at Stew's. You can do the same by either hiring a professional focus group company, or, like Stew Leonard's, conducting these meetings yourself. Stew Leonard, Jr., offers these ideas to make your Saturday morning meetings a success:

- *Invite 15 customers.* Expect 2 to 5 no-shows leaving you a group of 10 to 12.
- *Have 2 to 6 managers attend.* This creates a healthy ratio of custom ers to managers and shows a businesswide interest in customer feedback.
- *Reward customer participation.* Stew provides $20 gift certificates.
- *Don't evaluate ideas on the spot.* During the meeting, every idea is a good idea. This keeps people talking.
- *Type up all ideas.* Transcribe ideas within an hour and distribute them to all managers, then follow up.[5]

800 Numbers—Making It Easy

The first commercial use of an 800 number was introduced in 1967 by Whirlpool Corporation. Whirlpool's customers could call the toll-free Cool Line®* service number for assistance on the operation, care and mainte-nance of their household appliances.

---

* Registered trademark of Whirlpool Corporation.

The Cool Line® service was retired in the early 1990s and replaced by a consumer feedback system that was truly state of the art. Whirlpool created two Consumer Assistance Centers. When a customer calls for help, Whirlpool's phone system and computer work together to:

- Identify the incoming phone number.
- Route the call to the representative that last spoke to the customer (if the customer called in the past 10 days).
- Place the complete profile of the customer on the representative's computer screen.

All this occurs *before the call is answered.* Using artificial intelligence technology and decision-tree computer programming, the Whirlpool representative can ask for symptoms, quickly narrow down the source of the problem, and suggest a specific solution.

Whirlpool customers undoubtedly appreciate the speed with which most problems can now be solved. But what they most appreciate is an easy way to be *heard.* Several studies on consumer behavior show that over 90 percent of all dissatisfied customers never complain, making it impossible for a business to recover. But Whirlpool's own research indicates that:

- 97 percent of customers who are heard and whose problems are solved will buy from Whirlpool again.
- 70–80 percent of those whose problem can't be solved but feel that someone at the center listened buy from Whirlpool again.[6]

Louisville, Kentucky, is the home of General Electric's GE Answer Center® service. Approximately 4 million calls are received a year asking questions ranging from, "How do I set the timer on my new microwave?" to, "I just froze my marbles in the ice maker. How can I get them out of the ice cubes before my Mom gets home?" Consumer representatives work from a database of over a million possible questions and answers to satisfy customers' needs.

The GE Answer Center® number is easy to find. It's in product manuals, TV and print advertising, and 600 phone books nationwide. And the center never sleeps. Calls are answered 24 hours a day, seven days a week.

Bill Waers, director of the Answer Center service, knows the operation is not an expense item for the company but a money-maker. GE's research shows that 80 percent of customers who have a problem and bring it to

GE's attention will buy from GE again. Only 10 percent of those who don't speak up are repeat buyers.[7]

The Coca-Cola Company learned the value of an 800 number when they introduced a newly formulated version of Coke®* in 1985. The company was in the process of replacing the original Coke with this new version when the phone began to ring. And ring. And ring.

At its peak, 12,000 Coke drinkers were calling the toll free number to comment on the reformulation. The Coca-Cola Company had carefully researched consumers' preference for the taste of new Coke. What they hadn't measured was their consumers' emotional and nostalgic attachment to the original product. The calls helped the company readjust its marketing plan to keep consumers satisfied.

Roger Nunley, director of industry and consumer affairs at Coca-Cola USA, shares these ideas on recovery:

• *Over*compensate the consumer who's experienced quality problems. For example, if a consumer calls and is dissatisfied with two cans of Coke, she'll receive a coupon for a free six-pack. If you own a restaurant and the customer receives a bad entree, replace the entree *and* offer a free dessert.

• Satisfactorily resolving conflicts is good business. Eighty-five percent of consumers who are satisfied with the resolution of their complaint continue to purchase products of The Coca-Cola Company at preproblem levels. In fact, almost 10 percent of satisfied complainers actually purchase *more* of the company's products than they did prior to experiencing a problem.[8]

The telephone is the fastest, most efficient way to gather customer feedback. If you decide to create a toll-free hot line, make sure it's answered by a human being 24 hours a day. If your customer calls after 5 PM and listens to a recording, he'll question how serious you are about listening to him.

Toll-free numbers are also a great way to capture the creative juices of your customers and to discover customer-pleasing ways to improve your product or service. Good ideas from customers should be rewarded. Ask for the customer's address and send her a small item displaying your company logo, perhaps a key chain or a tote bag. This builds loyalty and encourages your innovative customers to call you again when other brainstorms erupt.

---

*Coca-Cola and Coke are registered trademarks of The Coca-Cola Company.

Reach Out and Surprise Someone

The two most effective recovery tools are you and your telephone. Why wait for complaint calls to come in? Why not call out looking for them?

Many dentists are masters at this technique. Patients who have recently undergone major work are called and asked, "Is everything OK? I just wanted to check to see if you're recovering well." The patient may not have fond memories of the procedure but is sure to appreciate the time and effort made by the dentist.

You need not be in the root canal business to make this idea work for you. Simply collect a list of recent customers and call each of them asking if they're satisfied with your product or service. The benefits are:

- The customer who is called and is dissatisfied is more likely to provide you with feedback than if he were not called.
- Dissatisfaction is captured before being spread to other potential customers.
- It provides you the opportunity to recover on the spot.
- The call is a pleasant surprise. The satisfied customer will be im pressed with your extra effort.
- You impress the customer even if you don't speak to her. Just leaving a detailed message on the customer's answering machine shows you took the time to follow up.
- Until all businesses routinely make this practice a habit, you're outdistancing your competition.

When GTE, the telecommunications company, acquired Contel a few years ago, they received more than a business. Some great ideas came with the acquisition. One was the habit of contacting every new business telephone installation to ensure that the customer was satisfied with the work. Any dissatisfaction was quickly captured and recovered.

Many car owners express amazement at the salesperson who calls every few months to see if their car is still running well. If your car salesperson called you and your car *was* running well, where would you go for *your* next car?

BETTER NOW THAN LATER

Feedback is not like wine, cheese, or people. It does not get better with age. The most effective feedback is instant. Let's return to the restaurant you were visiting and let's assume you've been served a bad piece of fish. Which of the following feedback methods gives the restaurant the best chance to *recover* your business?

- A mailed questionnaire or research phone call received two weeks after the meal?
- A comment card filled out and dropped in a box on your way out the door?
- A waiter who asks you during the meal if you are satisfied?

The answer should be clear. Recovery is a transformation process where the goal is to encourage the dissatisfied customer to talk to you, not his friends and business associates. The more quickly the feedback is received the better the chance that the customer's business can be recovered.

The comment card will teach you how to do better the next time, but you'll probably be doing better with a different customer.

The mailed questionnaire is the vehicle most likely to make it comfortable for the customer to complain, but the recovery process gets more complex and expensive. Winning the customer back now will take more than another serving of fish. Even if you do win the customer back, it may occur *after* the customer has spoken to other potential customers about the bad experience.

That's why it is so important to teach your customer contact employees to uproot misunderstandings or dissatisfaction while conducting business. Questions must be asked with genuine concern—you can't afford to sound robotic. Robotic questions tend to attract robotic customer responses.

If a waiter approaches you and asks mechanically, "How is everything?" You may respond "Fine," even if things are *not* fine. Both the waiter's attitude and the structure of the question discourage honest feedback. It's easier to respond "Fine" to the waiter and to provide your honest feedback to friends and neighbors after you leave.

The waiter genuinely concerned with your satisfaction should ask, "Are you enjoying your meal?" or "Is everything OK?" Here you're being asked a question designed to elicit either "Yes, I'm satisfied" or "No, I'm not satisfied." More recovery opportunities are created.

If you're not a restaurateur, try these questions to help uncover any hidden dissatisfaction:

- "Is there anything else I can help you with today?"
- "Have I answered all of your questions?"

Have I Answered Your Question?

One of the great challenges of telephone contact is that you can't *see* if a customer is satisfied. You can compensate for the lack of this visual comment card. If a customer asks you a question over the phone and there is any doubt in your mind as to whether the customer has either understood or is satisfied with your answer, follow up your answer with this question: "Have I answered your question?"

Many customers avoid confrontation. They may have no idea what you just said but won't tell you for fear of appearing foolish. The result is that questions go unasked or unanswered and the seeds of discontent grow. Like the questions suggested for the waiter, "Have I answered your question?" invites a yes or no response. It gives permission for the customer to say, "No, you lost me midway through your explanation. Could you explain it again?" You'll create greater satisfaction and eliminate unnecessary confusion.

Silence is deadly to a business. Quiet customers don't help you get better. Quiet dissatisfied customers take their business elsewhere. That's why it is so important for you to deliver it right the first time and to create a feedback system for those times when you don't. Remember, if customers don't talk, they walk.

AVOIDABLE RECOVERY SITUATIONS

Here are the two most common situations and how to avoid them.

Unexpected bills. When a customer asks you how much your product or service will cost, either be accurate or offer a not-to-exceed estimate. There should be no costs beyond what you quote.

Let's say you're a physician and you have a patient who's not feeling well. You order a procedure and the patient asks you how much the procedure will cost. Be sure to include *all* costs the patient will incur in your quote—your fee, the hospital fees, and the laboratory fees. To provide less than the full cost is to create a situation where your patient pays *your* bill and believes his bill paying is over. One week later, a bill arrives from some out-of-state laboratory. Suddenly, he's not feeling well again.

If you offer repair work on items other than the human body, the same advice applies—no surprises. Your customer should be informed up front what you will charge. Don't wait for customers to ask.

When my wife and I first moved into our home, we decided we'd like to purchase a gas clothes dryer. Shortly after we moved, we saw a gas dryer at a garage sale. The price? Fifteen dollars. How could we lose? We did.

The gas line entering the basement needed to be extended in order to reach the location of the dryer. We called a local heating and plumbing contractor who sent two men over to do the job. The sounds emanating from the basement gave the impression that these men were involved in a major archeological dig. Occasionally, one of the them would come upstairs and announce he was going to get a part. By lunchtime, the job was completed. I was asked to sign a work order. No pricing information was listed.

Two weeks later, the bill arrived. Our subterranean visitors had charged us $309, more than 20 times the cost of the dryer! And that's not the end of the story. We later discovered that our garage sale dryer ran only on propane, not on natural gas. It was the worst $15 investment we ever made.

The contractor attempted to recover by offering to slightly reduce the bill. We paid the bill, but we haven't used his services since.

When this example is used in seminars, some attendees say, "You should have asked for an estimate before the work began." I wasn't that smart. But even without asking, the situation could have been avoided. The best repair businesses teach their staff to *volunteer* an estimate.

Errors and omissions. Customers become frustrated when they place an order and the wrong items are received. So many possible mistakes can be made—wrong size, color, or quantity, or even the wrong item. The best way to ensure accuracy is to repeat the order back to your customer. This gives the customer the chance to catch any mistakes before the call is completed. It also shows your customer how interested you are in getting it right, right from the start.

THE TRANSFORMATION

When a customer calls a problem to your attention, you move into the recovery mode. Ask, "What exactly is wrong with the product?" "Please tell me specifically how we let you down." This information serves a vital role in the future success of your business. If the customer tells you how you've disappointed her, you can avoid disappointing other customers in the future.

Next, ask the customer how she'd like the problem solved. "What could I do to completely resolve this matter?" The customer's solution may be one that you would never consider.

One woman in Massachusetts was thrilled when she drove out of the automobile dealership with her family in their brand new car. The next day, the car wouldn't start. The car was towed to the dealer and the service department determined the problem was the SMEC (single-module engine controller), which oversees all the electronic functions of the engine. "We'll have to order a new SMEC," she was told. "It will take at least a week for it to come in."

"But we're starting our vacation the day after tomorrow and we want to take our new car."

"I can't see what else we can do," responded the serviceman. The customer could. "Don't you have any other new cars on the lot that use one of those SMECs? Why couldn't you take one out of the other car and put it in mine?" Two days later, off she drove with her family for two weeks of fun and sun—in their new car. Your customer may create a solution that provides total satisfaction and completes the recovery process.

Recovery Requires Speed

When clean, simple solutions are not possible, it's essential that you move out of a business-as-usual mode and provide unusual service. To do less is to tempt the customer to start looking elsewhere.

Take a mail-order company as an example. Let's say a loyal customer calls and says, "Where's my order? I wanted that item for my son's birthday." The customer service representative might find no record of the order and offer to send the item as soon as possible.

That's not fast enough. If a customer's order is misplaced or lost or if the wrong item was shipped using surface mail, the correct item should be sent a faster way.

A customer who takes the time to write a letter of criticism deserves more than a letter in return. Pick up the phone, call directory assistance, and then call the customer. Save your form letters for routine business. There's a customer's future business at stake. It's an *opportunity*. Grab the phone and take advantage of it.

Recovery Requires Constant Updates

Recovery is more likely when you keep customers informed throughout the process.

"I'll call you back by the end of the day." Keep this promise. If you reach an answering machine, leave as detailed an update as you can.

It's tempting in a moment of zeal to say, "I'll get *right* back to you." You've almost guaranteed failure to recover. The most common interpretation of "I'll get right back to you" is, "You can sit by your phone and wait for it to ring." You've created an unrealistic expectation and placed undue pressure on yourself.

It's better to set realistic expectations and exceed them than to set unrealistic expectations and compound the problem.

"I don't have any additional information yet, but I'll call you as soon as I do." This is known as the *no-news call.* If you tell someone you'll get back to them by the end of the day with a resolution to a problem and the end of the day arrives without a solution, *call the customer anyway.* A customer would rather receive no news than no call.

How to remember. Keep your promises to follow up by developing methods to remind you of important follow-up calls on very busy days:

• *Buy an alarm watch.* Set the alarm to go off 10 minutes before the time you promised to call your customer back. This makes it impossible to leave work without touching base with the customer. The watch will remind you to call; it's up to you to remember *whom* to call!

• *Leave yourself a voice mail.* If your office has voice mail, you can use it to talk to yourself: "Don't forget to call Sally Jones at 555-1234. You promised you'd call her by 2 PM."

• *Use memory resident software.* Some scheduling/appointment software will pop up a message reminding you to call a customer. The message will appear even if you're working in a different application.

Recovery Requires Teamwork

Establish a companywide term for *recovery opportunities.* You might call them *ROs* for short. When leaving messages for a co-worker, label your request as an RO. Make it clear what your timetable is, that is, when your customer expects a response. This should motivate your co-workers to give your request high priority.

If you keep the customer informed throughout the recovery process and produce a satisfactory resolution you can:

• Create additional customers. When a customer feels you've made heroic efforts to solve his problem, he tells others about the experience and becomes your most effective salesperson.

• Create a more loyal customer. The customer who feels that you've done more than correct the problem, that you've somehow compensated for the inconvenience, is more likely to spurn your competitors and continue to do business with you.

The Case of the Red Slippers

L. L. Bean, Inc., of Freeport, Maine, is famous for its efforts to keep customers satisfied and recover those who aren't. An L. L. Bean customer purchased a pair of red slippers. One rain-soaked morning he stepped outside in his slippers to retrieve his newspaper. Afterward, he walked across the white shag carpet in his living room only to discover that the rug showed evidence of his path. The red dye had run off his slippers onto the rug.

The customer called L. L. Bean and explained what had happened. The L. L. Bean customer service representative arranged for a local rug cleaning company to visit the customer's home and remove the stains to the customer's complete satisfaction. Had the stains not come out, L. L. Bean was prepared to replace the rug. A pretty expensive way to run a business?

No, a pretty *smart* way to do business. L. L. Bean lost the profit on that sale, but look at the other consequences:

• The customer, convinced that L. L. Bean stood behind its products, probably bought more L. L. Bean products.

• The customer helped the company discover they were producing an unsatisfactory product. They could correct the production problem and prevent future similar recovery situations.

• Research shows that most customers in this situation will tell at least half a dozen friends about that great company in Maine that arranged to have the rug cleaned.[9]

• New names were probably added to L. L. Bean's mailing list.

Saturn and the Defective Engine Coolant

One customer drove into his Saturn dealer in Westbrook, Maine, and reported that his new car was losing engine coolant. The service department replaced the coolant and then used its satellite link to report the problem to company headquarters in Spring Hill, Tennessee. The next day, another customer pulled into the Westbrook dealership with a similar problem.

More than five reports of coolant problems had now reached Spring Hill. This triggered an alert in the computerized service file and the Saturn recovery experts swung into action. Within hours, the problem had been isolated to one specific supply of coolant, and Saturn knew 1,836 cars had been affected. Saturn decided not to replace the coolant or the cooling systems. They decided to replace the cars.[10]

Customers received an overnight letter asking them to visit the dealership to order their new vehicle.[11] Some customers were reimbursed for rental cars for a day while waiting for their new car to arrive. One couple, John and Davina Manna, decided not to wait for an exact duplicate of their original Saturn and opted for a car right off the lot. The new car had a sunroof. Their original Saturn hadn't. Saturn threw in this $530 option for free.

Michael Salerno, vice president of Saturn of Jersey City, New Jersey, reports that the next day he sold two cars on the news that Saturn was replacing, not fixing, the cars.[12]

Going the Extra Mile

Some would argue that Saturn's replacing cars rather than cooling systems was a bad business decision. In the short term, the expense was high. But Saturn knew that attempting to save a few dollars now might cost them plenty of dollars in lost sales in the future. This was a risk the company was not willing to take. Splitting hairs with a customer is a fast way to lose him for good.

Within the past five years, I've had experiences with two defective products. The contrast in the two companies' responses will be instructive.

After only 30,000 miles on our car, we discovered that its tires were almost completely worn. Stopping by a store franchised by the tire manufacturer, I inquired whether any problems had been reported on the tires in question. The service manager pulled out a large three-ring binder and began to read a service bulletin. It was about my tires on my vehicle. The bulletin explained that because of a defect in the rubber compound of these tires, they were subject to premature wear unless properly aligned and frequently rotated.

The dealer offered to prorate the tires if they were found defective.

Three years ago, I bought a pair of running shoes made by the Hyde Athletic Shoe Company. After running in the shoes for over a month, I began to develop pain in one of my hips. Upon inspecting the shoes, I discovered that one of the outer soles appeared to be out of alignment with the upper. I called Hyde and they asked me to return the shoes for inspection. In less than a week I had received a brand new pair of shoes at no charge.

Hyde didn't ask me how many miles I had put on the shoes. The shoes weren't prorated. The company recognized the shoes were defective and was willing to pay the price. The business was recovered.

It's unfortunate the tire company wasn't willing to take an L. L. Bean, Saturn, or Hyde Athletic Shoe approach. Until or unless they become the only tire manufacturer in the world, we'll buy our tires elsewhere.

Avoiding the cost of complete recovery saves you money only in the short term. Down the road, you pay in bad word of mouth and lost business. Furthermore, it costs you much more to find a new customer than to recover an existing one.[13]

Tale of One City

Two Milwaukee, Wisconsin–based businesses were confronted with recovery opportunities. One recovered, one did not.

Harley-Davidson, the motorcycle maker, is a survivor and a thriver in a fiercely competitive business. But to Harley owners, there is no competition. In his book, *Well Made in America— Lessons From Harley Davidson on Being the Best*, Peter C. Reid writes:

> From its first appearance in 1903, the Harley motorcycle has been unique. . . . To Harley owners, Harleys have heart, Harleys have soul. . . . It's a feeling that many cannot articulate, and for them there's a Harley T-shirt inscribed: "Harley-Davidson —If I Have to Explain, You Wouldn't Understand."[14]

This loyalty was severely tested in the 1970s. Though the bikes retained their unique styling, quality had run right off the road. In 1974, Ray Tritten was assigned by Harley's then-parent company, AMF, to revive the product and discovered that Harley had grown unresponsive to complaints from dealers and customers. Nearly every motorcycle delivered to dealers had to be thoroughly serviced before it would run.[15]

The company's major turnaround came several years later, in 1983. Quality had improved tremendously but even customers who wanted to believe in Harley had to be recovered. Harley created the SuperRide program. New prospects and former loyal customers were offered demonstration rides at motorcycle events and dealerships. Riders could see for themselves the bikes no longer vibrated or leaked oil. Harley also acknowledged past quality problems with a print advertisement that said, "Thank God They Don't Leak Oil Anymore."[16]

In the same year, the company created HOG (Harley Owners Group), which organizes rallies in every region of the country.[17] These events provided Harley with the perfect chance to ask customers, "What should we do?" and "How are we doing?"

While Harley-Davidson was recognizing its need to recover its straying customers, a brewery across town was riding a new wave of popularity. Fueled by effective advertising and excellent rapport with beer wholesalers, it became the second most popular beer in the United States.

Then came the mistake. The brewery introduced a new brewing technique known as agitated fermentation. Stirring the brew accelerated the fermentation process allowing the brewery to produce more beer in less time.

It wasn't just the beer that became agitated. Wholesalers, distributors, and field representatives complained to headquarters that the beer's taste had changed. A fine sediment would collect at the bottom of the bottle if the beer was stored for more than a few weeks. The brewery, so intent on continuing its efficient method of production, failed to listen to its customers and sales plummeted.

The new brewing method was eventually discarded and the original method reinstated. But it was too late. Once-loyal consumers refused to be recovered. At this writing, the beer is still produced but has never come close to attaining its former market share.

Wherein lies the difference?

• *Harley listened and responded.* Harley took customers' concerns seriously, corrected quality problems, got the message out to customers, and created a feedback system to ensure history would not repeat itself. The brewery, ignoring reports of deteriorating quality, chose a less comprehensive response and watched its brand loyalty evaporate.

• *Harley's product was distinct.* No motorcycle looked or sounded like a Harley. Its customers were strongly inclined to return to the product because it could be obtained nowhere else. The beer drinker making his purchase just pulled a different brand off the shelf.

Many businesses think their customers see them as a Harley-Davidson when they'd be better off assuming their customers see them as just another brand of beer. Customer loyalty is earned in the marketplace every single business day.

If you want your customer reaching for *your* brand, find out what he wants, ask him how you're doing, and jump through hoops when you let him down.

Here are the three ideas from this chapter that I will use right away:

1. _____

2. _____

3. _____

Chapter Six

Resolving Conflicts

Gossip is when you hear something you like about someone you don't.
Earl Wilson

Do you remember the childhood game of telephone? You sat in a circle with other children and the first child whispered a secret to the child on his right. After a few giggles, the second child turned to her right and whispered the secret to the next child. The process was repeated until the secret had made a full circle.

Do you remember what happened to the original secret by the end of the circle? How could it bear so little resemblance to what was whispered last? It must have been because all of the communicators were children, right?

Wrong. Adults play the same game in the workplace, with identical short-term results. Information gets mangled. The game of telephone is harmless when played by children but takes on dangerous implications in the hands of adults.

Walk down any public path, sit on any park bench, visit any company lunch-room and you're sure to hear all kinds of people discussing the same topic—other people. When an individual is embroiled in a major co-worker conflict, he will seek out the sympathetic ear of anyone or anything before he'll make the effort to confront the co-worker. He'll tell his best friend, other co-workers, his barber, even his dog, before he'll approach the one person who could help him solve his problem.

When people speak *about* each other, the job's not getting done. When people speak *to* each other, conflicts are resolved and the focus returns to serving customers. Supervisors should teach staff to engage in the art of constructive confrontation. Employees should also learn how to respond when caught between two feuding co-workers.

Counselors practicing transactional analysis use this triangle to describe what often occurs in both domestic and workplace disputes:

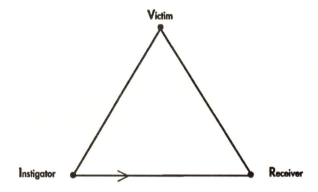

Letter *I* grows frustrated in her dealings with the person represented by the Letter *V*. Avoiding a confrontation, she turns to Letter *R* and vents to him.

Letter *R*, known as the *receiver*, has several options:

- He can go to Letter *V*, the *victim*, and tell the victim what Letter *I*, the *instigator*, has said about her.
- He can try to get the victim and instigator together to discuss and solve their conflict.
- He can move outside the triangle and tell some totally new person what he's just heard. This is how the game of telephone begins. Round and round it goes; where it ends, no one knows.

The receiver does have one other option, the one most often recommended by professional counselors. He can turn to the instigator and say:

- "Does Letter *V* (the victim) know you're saying this?"
- "Does Letter *V* know you feel this way?"

This is his nonjudgmental way of saying, "Communicating this frustration to me brings you no closer to resolving your conflict. Why don't you talk to the person with whom the conflict exists?" It's the best way to stop potential gossip in its tracks and to ensure the game of telephone is canceled due to lack of interest.

There are two types of workplace conflicts we'll discuss:

- *A major personality conflict.* Two people are working shoulder to shoul der and are at each other's throats. They're so busy being angry at each other that the customer isn't being served.
- *Minor workplace frustrations.* Nerves occasionally fray due to indi vidual idiosyncracies. Employees like each other, but on certain days, drive each other crazy.

MAJOR PERSONALITY CONFLICTS

Major personality conflicts can be extremely difficult to resolve. Learning and practicing some basic interpersonal skills can help you tip the odds in your favor.

First, recognize that major personality conflicts can sometimes be arrested before they develop. Employees who constructively confront one another in the early stage of frustration can talk through a situation and uproot a conflict before it grows.

Second, let's make a clear distinction between a major personality conflict and minor workplace frustrations. Minor workplace frustrations make you shake your head; major personality conflicts make you lose sleep. Minor workplace frustrations are usually forgotten by the end of the day; major personality conflicts never leave you. You wake up each morning dreading the day because of that certain you-know-who. You're dwelling on the co-worker rather than the needs of the customer.

Here's a step-by-step method to resolve a major personality conflict so both of you can get back to work:

1. *Write it down.* Use a pen and paper to expose how you're feeling about the conflict. Writing is a remarkable form of expression. It helps you identify and clarify your feelings. You begin to feel better because you're getting your emotional house in order. For example, have you ever written a letter to someone and not sent it, and yet felt it was a very productive use of your time?

What you've written can serve another useful purpose. It can be your vehicle of communication when you approach your co-worker. You might feel intimidated when dealing with this individual. If you rely on the spoken word, you might express yourself less completely than you do on paper. Before approaching the co-worker, you can write it down, tear it up, write it again, and continue the process until you feel that what you see on the paper is exactly what you have on your mind.

When it's time to express yourself to the co-worker, you can hand what you've written to him with full assurance that what you intended to say will be communicated.

2. *Approach the co-worker.* Not just any approach will work. The most effective technique is the one that's most difficult because it runs counter to your emotional instincts. Here are the three possible approaches—from least effective to most effective:

- "I've got a problem and you're it, so *listen to me.*"
- "There seem to be some bad vibes between you and me. *Let's talk* about what we can do about it."
- "I know I'm not always the easiest person to deal with. *Tell me* how my behavior is affecting your work."

Listen to me. The blame for this conflict is now being laid at the doorstep of your co-worker. It's the other person who is 100 percent at fault, so why not just jump right in and start persuading your co-worker how wrong he is? Besides, what would your co-worker have to say that would be of value?

Instead of building a foundation for a discussion, you're launching a monologue. This listen-to-me approach says to your co-worker, "I am not interested in what *you* have to say, only in expressing myself." Your co-worker develops an acute, temporary hearing loss.

This method is popular with frustrated parents. Children hear Mom or Dad say, "Now you listen to me . . ." If you were the child, how interested would you be in what was about to be said?

Let's talk. Using the pronouns *we* and *our* indicates your willingness to accept some responsibility for the conflict. You don't see the conflict as a zero-sum game. Perhaps your behavior is part of the reason the two of you find yourselves in this situation. This approach can be most useful in resolving minor workplace misunderstandings. It's informal and unthreatening.

Tell me. Inviting your co-worker to express himself first indicates an equal interest in understanding his point of view and being understood. You build a foundation of trust that allows true dialogue to occur.

This idea has been advocated for centuries. If you recite the Prayer of St. Francis, you ask, "May I be more interested in understanding than in being understood." Over 40 years ago, psychotherapist Carl Rogers broke new ground in business thinking in a *Harvard Business Review* article. He advocated businesspeople learn to listen to others with understanding, rather than personal judgment.[1]

More recently, Stephen Covey urges the same approach in his book, *The Seven Habits of Highly Effective People.* One of Covey's habits is: Seek first to understand, then to be understood.[2] He describes the value of empathic listening—listening for feelings and restating or reporting these feelings back to the other person.

Carl Rogers makes this suggestion:

> Here's one way to test the quality of your understanding. The next time you get into an argument with your spouse, friend, or small group of friends, stop the discussion for a moment and suggest this rule: "Before each person speaks up, he or she must *first* restate the ideas and feelings of the previous speaker accurately and to that speaker's satisfaction."[3]

This is *not* easy. It's no coincidence that this virtue was high on St. Francis' prayer list! But by opening your ears and eyes to the ideas and feelings of the other person, you strongly motivate your co-worker to listen and understand *your* ideas and feelings.

You take a deep breath, approach this co-worker, and say, "Things don't seem to be working out between the two of us. I'd like to give you the chance to tell me how my behavior might be affecting your work. I'd then like to tell you my feelings. Can we meet sometime soon?" Exhale and wait for your co-worker's response.

3. *Meet with the co-worker.* If he agrees to meet, establish a mutually convenient time and consider meeting away from the business. Otherwise, news of your meeting might create a new game of telephone in your workplace.

If you do meet on-site, do it in a *neutral location.* Meeting in your work space or his can affect the dynamics of the meeting. The less intimidation, the better.

You would first invite your co-worker to express himself: "Please tell me how my behavior is interfering with your ability to do your job."

Listen. You may discover personal shortcomings that friends and co-workers have longed to tell you but were never given the chance. You will be tempted to interrupt. Resist the temptation. This is the time for two open ears and one closed mouth. When you feel you've understood what your co-worker has said, ask, "Is there anything else I should know?" Don't be surprised if there is more. Perhaps your co-worker has waited a long time for this opportunity. Continue to ask, "Is there anything else I should know?" until the response is no. Now it's your turn to speak, right?

Not so fast. Don't forget the rule suggested by Carl Rogers. Next, summarize what you've just heard from your co-worker. "Have I understood you?" When the answer is yes, you move to the next step—expressing yourself.

You may choose to speak your concerns or to hand your co-worker what you've written. In either case, most counselors recommend that you describe your co-worker's behavior and then describe how you feel in the presence of that behavior. It would sound like this: "When you act this way, this is how I feel."

No guilt is assessed or intended. You're not saying *you make me feel. . .* To do so will simply put the other person on the defensive. Another person's behavior may act as a stimulus, but your emotional response is in large measure chosen, rather than predetermined.

You next ask your co-worker to summarize what you've said. If you're not satisfied that you've been understood, express yourself again and repeat the process. Now it's time to commit to action. Both of you should write down an equal number of behavioral changes you'll make to improve the working relationship. You should meet within a week to assess what progress has been made. Continue to schedule meetings until you both feel they're no longer necessary.

All of these ideas are contingent upon your co-worker's willingness to meet. Maybe he's unwilling. This is when it is necessary to ask for help from your supervisor.

The supervisor should see her role as a *mediator*, rather than a problem solver. She arranges a meeting with the two feuding employees. Once again the meeting should be held in a neutral location, *not in the supervisor's office*.

Let's say that John and Mary, both customer service representatives, are acting like the Hatfields and the McCoys. Their supervisor turns to Mary and says, "Mary, I want you to tell John how his behavior is affecting your work." Mary expresses her feelings. The supervisor asks, "Is there anything else John should know?"

The supervisor then asks John to repeat back what Mary has said and asks Mary whether she feels understood. Notice that the supervisor *does not* present the summation. Her job is to simply channel the discussion.

Satisfied that Mary has fully expressed herself and has been understood, the supervisor then turns to John and says, "I'd like you to tell Mary how her behavior is affecting your work." She probes John to ensure he has fully expressed himself, turns to Mary for a summation, and then verifies that John feels fully understood.

The supervisor will now help us reach the denouement of our drama by turning to both co-workers and asking: "How are you two going to resolve this situation?"

The process of mediation means insisting that the two conflicting parties create their own solution. This provides both employees with an important responsibility and a strong sense of ownership. Supervisors who concoct and impose solutions diminish the chance that a solution will take root.

Equal numbers of behavioral changes should be expected of both and committed to writing. A follow-up meeting should be scheduled so that progress can be assessed. Meetings should be scheduled until all three parties consider them no longer necessary.

MINOR WORKPLACE FRUSTRATIONS

A paradoxical thing happens when companies conduct job satisfaction surveys. Employees are asked, "What do you like *most* about your job?" One of the most frequent responses is, "The people with whom I work." Employees are then asked, "What do you like *least* about your job?" One of the most frequent responses is, you guessed it, "The people with whom I work."

We human beings are social animals. We enjoy each other's company. But sometimes we drive each other crazy. Anyone who has ever had a brother or sister, a roommate, or a spouse will fully understand. What is the best way to cope with the anxiety-inducing habits of our co-workers?

Perhaps you turn to a different co-worker and say, "You know what she does that drives me right up the wall?" With your luck, you'll pick a well-read co-worker who will say:

- "Does she know you feel this way?"
- "Does she know you're saying this?"

More likely, you'll begin a new game of telephone. No one can imagine what your initial comment will be when it reaches the end of the circle.

Instead, stop and assess whether you need to discuss this with the person driving you crazy. Is it affecting your ability to serve your customers? Are the two of you on your way to a major personality conflict or is the irritation intermittent? If it is affecting your work or you feel you're heading towards a conflict, use a *let's talk* approach to clear the air.

If the irritation is infrequent, why not try this? Wait. By the end of the day, the minor irritation may have disappeared. Your silent tongue and sense of maturity may assure that the workplace remains harmonious. But if the end of the day comes and you still feel the need to talk about it, take it home and talk about it there.

When I first begin to suggest this idea in seminars, some heads shake no. "You should leave your work at work and go home and forget about it," some say. But I doggedly defend this idea because of what happened in one of the very first seminars I ever presented.

The program was conducted for a heating oil company that had been in business for over 110 years. Looking around the room, it seemed that some of the service technicians had been there almost that long. Most sat in the back row, arms folded, with a facial expression that seemed to say, "What's this young guy going to tell me that I don't already know?"

All morning, the expressions remained unchanged. At midafternoon, I introduced the idea of talking about your workday at home. One of those silent technicians raised his hand and announced to the room, "This is the most important thing he's said all day."

He had the group's attention. He then explained to his colleagues that he and his wife had raised five children. Successfully. He said one of the secrets to their success was that they always made the effort to eat one meal a day as a family. Everyone in the family had the chance to share a brief report on his or her day. He continued, "Everyone in your house has the need to answer the question, 'How was your day? How was work? How was school? How was play?'"

It was one of the most effective sales presentations I had ever seen. So I folded my arms and listened. What followed was a spirited discussion in the group about how helpful it is to share the small victories and minor defeats of work with those people we love. Here are some of the advantages they listed:

• You avoid the workplace game of telephone.
• Your loved ones love you, not your company, and can offer more dispassionate suggestions than your co-workers.
• Your loved ones may reveal the humor in your predicament and persuade you to "lighten up."

If you want to make this *"dinner table review"* even more effective, try these suggestions:

• No TV, radio, newspapers, or magazines. Completely clear the eating area of any visual distractions.
• Shut off the ringer on your telephone. Let an answering machine take messages. This time belongs to you and your loved ones. The friends and the telemarketers can wait.

If you live alone, pick up the telephone and share your day with someone who cares. Don't forget that the person listening to you would love for you to return the favor.

Using this off-site outlet and the other ideas in this chapter help provide you with an emotional spring cleaning. You'll find that you arrive at the job disinclined to gossip and more anxious to get to work. And when co-workers are no longer adversaries, you'll begin to treat them like customers. Ideas on how to serve them more effectively are found in the next chapter.

Here are the three ideas from this chapter that I will use right away:

1. _____

2. _____

3. _____

Chapter Seven

Inside Customers

Imagine you're in a helicopter traveling above a long, winding river. Looking down, you notice that what you thought was a single large river is actually a product of many smaller streams that send water into the river. Each stream knows exactly where to flow. All share a common destination. Having received contributions upstream, the river completes the journey by emptying its contents into the ocean.

Let's take an aerial view of your business. Think of the delivery of your product as being like that river emptying into the ocean. The process is impossible without the upstream contributions of all of the people in your organization. Every creative idea in a brainstorming meeting, every request for help that is met, in short, each time your work flows into the work of your co-worker, you're improving the product the customer receives downstream.

You may never see or speak to this downstream customer, but your work is affecting someone who does. Everyone in an organization has two customers—the purchaser of your product, the *outside* customer, and the other employees of your organization, the *inside* customer.

When you adopt this way of thinking, every interaction with a co-worker becomes customer service. Requests from inside customers are handled with the same speed and efficiency as those received from outside customers. Too often, employees engage in a form of triage, giving emergency service to outside customers while placing inside customers on the back burner. Such prioritizing is dangerous because your inside customer may be attempting to serve the needs of an outside customer but is unable to do so until she hears from you.

A BUSINESS WITHIN A BUSINESS

Some departments think that providing customer service is a skill needed only in the customer service department. Because they're the only source for their special brand of expertise, they operate like their own little river.

Inside customers exposed to this cavalier attitude cut a new path and find ways to do business without them.

There are no monopolies within an organization. All departments face the silent, invisible competitor known as the "end around." For example, an unresponsive internal software support group may find that its phone stops ringing. An inflexible corporate purchasing department may discover that employees are making their purchases elsewhere. Enlightened departments avoid complacency. They're competing in the internal marketplace and strive to attract inside customers rather than build barriers that drive them away.

The best departments operate a successful business within a business. They establish speed guidelines for meeting customers' needs. They're constantly looking for ways to be an easier place to do business. They stay on target by regularly meeting with inside customers. The quality of their work is driven by the needs of those they serve. *Every important skill you use to help attract and keep outside customers can be used to serve the needs of inside customers.*

When a business fully dedicates itself to superb customer service, it is like a great river. It has, in the words of Earl Nightingale, "direction, power, economy, and speed." [1]

SERVE THE SAME SANDWICH

In the chapter on friendly service, you learned the value of building a business sandwich in every customer contact. To build a business sandwich with your inside customer:

- Deliver a friendly phone greeting.
- Make a smooth transition into the business.
- Provide a friendly exit with an offer of future assistance.

Your phone greeting should include:

- The name of your department.
- "My name is . . .
- *How* may I help you?"

If you're unable to determine whether your calls originate from inside or outside customers, use the greeting appropriate for an *outside* customer. Expecting informality, some inside customers may "talk over" your greeting and cut you off. Stay with it. Your outside customers appreciate knowing *where* you are and *who* you are.

VOICE MAIL AS GREETING

Properly used voice mail can be your friendly greeting and help you meet the needs of inside customers even when you're unavailable. Use these ideas to make the most of your time away from the phone:

• *Change your outgoing message daily.* This habit instantly elevates your level of service. When you say today's date at the beginning of your message and then say you're, "either away from my desk or on the phone right now," your inside customer *believes* you. He's more confident he'll hear back from you today.

You may find changing your voice mail message about as much fun as flossing your teeth. If so, prepare a script for yourself. It's much easier to read it off a page than to pull it out of your head.

• *Offer a safety valve.* Your message should include the name of another person in your department who can assist the inside customer should he require an immediate response.

• *Offer instructions on how to transfer to the safety valve.* Tell your customer how to reach this individual. A customer, whether inside or outside, should only have to place one phone call to make her needs known.

Sounds great, but what if your conscientious safety valve is also on the phone or away from his desk right now? Your customer begins to enter the phone mail zone. He starts to hear: "No one in this department really wants to speak to you or hear your concerns. You'll have to hang up and redial or leave a message for me, the safety valve, even if you had no intention of speaking to me in the first place."

In a perfect world, every department has a full-time safety valve to assure that every caller always has the option of speaking to a real live human being. If your world isn't this perfect, pair up with another individual in your department. You can serve as safety valves for one another. This allows an inside customer to transfer to a safety valve and, upon discovering the safety valve is unavailable, receive instructions on how to return to the originally intended employee's voice mail and leave a message.

When you're the safety valve and a customer reaches you, assess the customer's need and determine whether you can fill that need. If you decide the customer needs to communicate with your co-worker, offer to do one of the following:

• Take a message.
• Allow the person to leave a message on your co-worker's voice mail.

It's easier for you and usually better for the customer if she leaves a message on voice mail. This is an excellent time to use another idea from an earlier chapter, the *AT&T idea*. A customer, given two options, tends to choose the latter option, so make the leaving of a voice mail message the second option you suggest.

Judy's Idea

Judy Giordano, a manager of offices and telecommunications, discovered that some of her co-workers had Type A personalities and refused to wait to hear her entire voice mail message. Instead, they would "punch through" her outgoing message and leave a message of their own. This sometimes caused a major service bottleneck. For example, let's say Judy's message announces that, "I'll be on vacation for two weeks and won't be returning phone calls until I return from vacation." This important information was being missed by the Type As who could only wonder why Judy's service was slipping.

Judy decided to grab the attention of these anxious customers. She began her message this way: "Please listen to this entire message."[2] This was a tip-off to callers that what was about to be said was timely and important. Inside customers did less punching and more listening, receiving better service in the process.

Another employee placed his inside customers at a high state of alert by beginning his outgoing message with, "Attention!" Those customers who had been in the military probably stood up next to their phones. He had good reason for this unconventional opening. He was on a sabbatical for several months and didn't want customers to leave messages. By combining his "Attention!" with the offering of a safety valve, he was both informative and helpful.

"Please Tell Me How I Can Help You."

Make this request on every outgoing voice mail message. It motivates your inside customer to leave you a more complete, detailed message. The better the messages, the better the service you can provide. Detailed messages make it possible for you to return calls with answers and solutions rather than questions.

Detailed messages also make it possible for you to fill an inside customer's need *without ever speaking to him*. When you call back and reach the inside customer's voice mail, you can leave the information requested. Your co-worker can retrieve the information at his convenience. This "how" idea is the single most effective way to reap a substantial return on your company's voice mail investment.

Here's a sample of a great outgoing voice mail message:

> Hi, this is Sally Decker in accounts payable. Today is Tuesday, November 10, and I'm either on the phone or away from my desk. Please leave me a message telling me exactly *how* I can help you. If you need to speak to someone immediately, please dial John Brownell at extension 216 at the end of this message. Thank you.

TAKING GOOD MESSAGES

Taking good messages from an outside customer is an invaluable service to your inside customer. You can use the old-fashioned tools of paper and pencil in a newly effective way. Here's how:

1. *Provide the time and date of the call.* This helps your co-worker decide whether there's a need for a return call. Perhaps your co-worker has spoken to the customer in the meantime, making another call awkward and unnecessary.

2. *Get a phone number.* Callers who tell you, "She knows my number," may be deluding themselves. What if the person for whom the message is intended does *not* know the number? Or what if she's "on the road" at a pay phone retrieving your message?
The best way to make her more productive is to tell the caller, "She may know your number, but let me take it from you just to be safe."

3. *Best time to reach.* This reduces telephone tag. Ask your caller when he is most likely to be available for a return call.

4. *Assure the caller that you will deliver the message.* Do not assure the customer of a speedy return call unless you are absolutely certain it will happen. Only make promises that you know will be kept.

Speed Guidelines

It's useful for message takers to probe for the reason for an inside customer's call. Is he calling for help in recovering an outside customer? If so, the call should receive the highest priority. By contrast, your inside customer may be requesting information that won't be used until the middle of next month. Knowing the *why* behind each request helps you serve *all* of your customers more effectively.

If an inside customer calls and leaves a message for you today, she should receive a return call from you today. While same-day solutions may not always be possible, same-day return phone calls are.

Lost and Found

Let's say that you decided to drive to a new state to visit an old friend. Approaching his town, you ascertain he's a better friend than a direction giver. You stop and ask a stranger for directions. Despite your great effort to follow this stranger's advice, you soon feel even more lost.
You drive up to a second stranger and ask *him* for directions. He says, "You know, I was just heading that way. How about if I hop in and take you there?" When a confused inside customer calls you, do you act more like the first stranger or the second? You can tell her any one of the following:

- "You're lost. You'll have to hang up and try again."
- "I'm not the place where you want to be. But let me try to give you some directions."
- "Let me take you there."

The same advice provided for dealing with outside customers applies in this case: *Take ownership for the customer's problem until the customer owns a solution.*

- Determine who inside your organization can serve this inside customer's needs.
- Transfer the call rather than insisting that the inside customer hang up and redial.
- Provide the name and extension number of the person to whom the call is about to be transferred.
- Offer your name and number should the inside customer have trouble reaching any individual in that department.

Excellent customer service sometimes requires going the extra mile for someone you don't even know. Each time you make the effort, you set an example for others and increase the chances that when you're lost, someone will go the extra mile for you.

THRIVING IN THE INTERNAL MARKETPLACE

Inside customers want to be heard and deserve the same opportunities to provide feedback afforded to outside customers. How well have you been listening lately? Does your inside customer have your ear? If so, you'll have her business. Don't wait for your inside customers to approach you. Reach out to them so they can better understand what you offer and how you can help.

One of our clients, an internal department of a large corporation, grew frustrated by the poor attendance at the meetings they had scheduled for their inside customers. I asked, "Where are these meetings held?" "Here in our department," was the response. Next I asked "When are these meetings held?" "They begin at 10 o'clock."

In other words, the customer was being asked to break up his workday and travel to this department's location to help the department do a better job. This is like a new potato chip company asking prospective customers to drive to the warehouse to sample a new product instead of offering free samples at the supermarket. Go where your customers are. Don't expect them to come to you.

The human resources department of a large hospital sets up a table outside the cafeteria so they can answer questions about employee benefits. Employees are provided a comfortable and time-efficient way to gather information.

A purchasing department introducing a new requisitioning software package decides to install a computer inside the company cafeteria so that employees can try out the software and informally ask questions. Not only has the department reached out, it's no longer a department, but people with names and faces and smiles.

EYEBALL TO EYEBALL/E-MAIL TO E-MAIL

Both of these departments learned that the most effective way to communicate is face to face. When you *visit* a customer, you communicate with:

• The words that you speak.
• The tone and inflection of your voice.
• Your facial gestures and body language.

When you contact your customer *by telephone*, you communicate with:

• The words you speak.
• The tone and inflection of your voice.

Notice the powerful tools of facial gestures and body language have been lost.

When you *send* your customer a memorandum or an electronic mail (E-mail) message, you communicate with:

• The words that you write.

In the movie *Star Wars*, Princess Leia Organa has a critical message for her ally, Obi-Wan Kenobi. She's been captured by the emperor's troops and needs Obi-Wan to ensure that the blueprints for the Death Star reach other members of the Rebel Alliance. She desperately wants her message to be heard.

Unable to deliver the message personally, she does the next best thing. She records a hologram message and sends it in the memory unit of the droid R2D2. Upon delivery, Obi-Wan watches a miniature image of the princess plead, "Help me Obi-Wan Kenobi. You're my only hope."

What would have happened if she had sent an E-Mail? Obi-Wan might not have paid attention. Instead she chose the power of words, facial expression, and body language to ensure her message was effectively conveyed.

Both memos and E-mail are highly imperfect communications tools and best reserved for the dissemination of routine information or as a backup for voice mail messages. When you need your customer's attention or cooperation, pick up the phone or, better still, pay the customer a visit.

In the most successful companies, everyone's a customer service representative. Employees not directly serving the customer buying the product are committed to serving the customer down the hall. In the long run, it's not powerful product innovations that help you outdistance your competition but what happens each day inside the walls of your workplace.

Here are the three ideas from this chapter that I will use right away:

1. _____

2. _____

3. _____

Chapter Eight

Finding and Keeping Good People

W hen I first speak to a job candidate, I'm looking for attitude," says Jill Tavello of Stew Leonard's Dairy in Norwalk, Connecticut. "We can teach job skills but it's almost impossible to make over a person's basic outlook."[1]

Bill Waers at the GE Answer Center service echoes Tavello's comments. He looks for a recent graduate's involvement in extracurricular activities as a strong indicator of the development of interpersonal skills.[2]

Walter Coleman, vice president of consumer services operations at Whirlpool Corporation, remarks, "There was a time years ago when we hired service employees with strong technical skills and figured that we'd teach them the people skills once they came on board. It didn't work."[3]

Training companies receive phone calls from managers who say, "I'd like you to do some work with our staff. We have a couple of people here who are really miserable with customers and we're hoping your seminars will change their attitudes." With this sole objective, the training program is purchased. But several months and many thousands of dollars later, the managers discover there's been no change in the behavior of the problem employees. This expensive lesson can be avoided. When hiring new employees, remember that a positive attitude should be a preexisting condition.

The best job interviewers imagine themselves as customers: "Would *I* want to do business with this person? Does he have some energy and enthusiasm in his voice? Is this conversation a pleasant give and take or am I being forced to do all the work?"

Jill Tavello uses the telephone as part of her screening interview. The candidate who shows no life over the phone is eliminated from consideration. At Stew Leonard's Dairy, every employee has daily customer contact or supports the efforts of someone who does. Energy and commitment must be present prior to employment or the individual will not contribute to the organization's success.

Whirlpool Corporation's current employee selection method is among the most sophisticated. In the late 1980s, Whirlpool formed a partnership with the Department of Psychology at the University of Notre Dame. Hiring became a customer-driven process. The first step was no longer interviewing job candidates but talking with customers. The goal of consumer research was to determine, "What are the satisfiers?" Customers were asked, "What kind of behavior must our staff present to keep you satisfied?"

Whirlpool calls these customer-inspired interpersonal skills *core behaviors*. Job applicants complete a questionnaire designed to help the company assess the job candidate's likeliness and willingness to provide these core behaviors. Customer involvement and quantitatively measured applicant responses have helped the company make better hiring decisions.[4] Because customer satisfaction is a moving target, Whirlpool's consumer research in this area is ongoing.[5]

REALITY CHECK

Once a good interviewer is convinced essential people skills are in place, the job candidate should try the job on for size. At Stew Leonard's, the prospective employee is taken to the floor of the store to experience firsthand what it's like to be approached by customers with questions or complaints. If the position being sought is in the meat department, the candidate will spend some time in the walk-in freezers and refrigeration units. If she wants to work in the bakery, Stew's wants to know: Can she stand the heat or does she need to get out of the kitchen? It's better for both the employer and the prospective employee to know *before* the hiring decision.

At Coca-Cola USA, prospective consumer assistance representatives spend time shoulder to shoulder with existing representatives listening to customer calls. They are also asked to participate in role plays of situations likely to occur on the job.[6]

Could you offer a similar job test-drive? Will the potential employee be expected to wear a telephone headset all day? Give him a headset to try out. Are your employees constantly on their feet? Conduct your second interview standing on the job floor with your applicant.

TEAM INTERVIEWING

Many companies involve a candidate's potential peers in the interviewing process. Several frontline employees at the GE Answer Center service have received interviewing training. They meet with applicants, answer questions, and share insights on what to expect on the job. Those making the final hiring decision benefit greatly from the impressions and feedback provided by the employees who are closest to the customer.[7]

There are four essential parts of any interviewing process:

1. *Screen for attitude.* Consider using Jill Tavello's telephone interview approach, especially if your new employee will be interacting with customers by telephone. A customer service manager recently told me, "I received a call from a prospective job applicant who sounded half-baked and half-awake. I made a point of writing down her name so I'd be sure *not* to hire her."

2. *Expose them to the work environment.* This is also the chance for other people in the organization to interview the candidate. Collect as many well-trained impressions and insights as possible. Peer input can be extremely valuable. Your best frontline people know what it takes to work effectively with customers. Ask for their help.

3. *Expose them to the work.* Create role-playing situations that help you determine the candidate's people skills and basic interpersonal instincts.

4. *Check references.* "Job applicants are often surprised to discover that we check all references," says Margaret Prager of Legal Sea Foods, Inc. " But we recognize that the employee will be an extension of the quality we work so hard to create and maintain. We don't want to make a mistake." Prager continues, "We also look for people who genuinely want to be in the service business, who are willing to make a commitment to the job and to our standards for quality and service. References can help us make that determination."[8]

HIRE IN BUNCHES

There's a tremendous advantage to hiring several employees simultaneously. Your training dollars are allocated more efficiently. For example, each new employee at GE's Answer Center service undergoes six weeks of intensive training prior to handling phone calls on her own. It's more cost-effective to schedule fewer training sessions with more people.

Hiring and training many employees simultaneously also creates teamwork and camaraderie. Consider all the children who move with their families to a new community in the middle of a school year. The youngster often feels a sense of classroom isolation or unacceptance. It's so much easier to arrive at the beginning of a school year when the new experience is shared by all students. The same holds true in the workplace. Being part of a new class engenders a connection with others. You "graduate" from a probationary period with someone else. You'll celebrate employment anniversaries together.

THE BUDDY SYSTEM

Pair up each new employee with a veteran. The seasoned employee can be the person who sits shoulder to shoulder with the newcomer during orientation. The mentoring employee is available to answer questions and to offer reassurance and encouragement. This relationship should not be scheduled to expire at some predetermined time. Such a mentor-mentee relationship can be perpetually and doubly beneficial.

SATISFIED EMPLOYEES CREATE SATISFIED CUSTOMERS

Writing in *The Harvard Business Review*, Leonard A. Schlesinger and James L. Heskett state, "The growing body of data we have collected thus far suggests that customer satisfaction is rooted in employee satisfaction and retention more than anything else."[9] Schlesinger and Heskett advocate an employee rather than a technological focus:

> Our data suggests as well that employee satisfaction is especially high in service organizations that not only deliver high value to customers but do it through frontline service workers who are carefully selected, well trained, given latitude to solve customer problems, compensated at least in part on their performance, and even given responsibility for ensuring that their positions are staffed.[10]

We know that Whirlpool Corporation identifies customer satisfiers and uses them to make better hiring decisions. Your company should take the next step. Identify employee satisfiers and make sure your managers exhibit the core behaviors that will drive *employee* satisfaction. Here are some of the satisfiers I've identified during a decade of listening to and observing frontline employees.

The Power of Praise

A former airline reservation agent told me, "When I was first hired, I was constantly told what a great job I was doing. During my orientation and probationary period, my manager sat next to me and listened to my phone calls. She offered excellent tips and constant feedback. Once my probationary period was over, she never sat with me again."

Once while leasing a new car, a sales representative asked me what I did for a living. After he learned of my work, he said, "I wish you could train our receptionist. The first two weeks she was here she was a ball of fire. I got more compliments about the way she answered our phone than anyone we had ever hired. Then it seemed overnight she changed. She has no life to her now. She doesn't show any enthusiasm when she picks up the phone. What do you think happened to her?"

I responded, "During those first several weeks when you were receiving all of those wonderful compliments about her work—did you ever share the compliments with *her?*" His long silence provided the answer.

William James once wrote, "The deepest principle of human nature is the craving to be appreciated."[11] The veracity of this behavioral principle isn't confined to the first two weeks on the job or the probationary period. An employee should feel appreciated from his first day of work to the night of his retirement party.

A Louis Harris & Associates, Inc., opinion survey conducted for *Business Week* asked employed adults: If you had to choose, which two or three of these factors are most important to you? Seven items were listed. Here are the top three vote getters:

- A good salary—63 percent.
- Job security—53 percent.
- Appreciation for a job well done—40 percent.[12]

Consultant Hanoch McCarty suggests you open a social bank account with each of your employees. Each time you praise your employee's performance, you're making a deposit. Every critical comment is a withdrawal. Your goal is to stay in the black and avoid being overdrawn.[13]

Stephen Covey describes this interpersonal process as the emotional bank account. Each time we contribute to another individual's self-esteem or keep our promises or praise a person's behavior, we build up reserves in the account. If the time comes to approach an individual about unacceptable performance, we can rely on reserves of trust and goodwill that have accumulated over time.[14]

The best way to make deposits is to create natural and regular ways to praise an employee's efforts. The ideal method is through shoulder-to-shoulder monitoring. Make it a habit to sit next to your employees who interact with customers over the telephone. Stand next to those who deal with customers on a walk-up basis. If your employees ride in a car or a truck, ride with them.

Plenty of businesses use shoulder-to-shoulder monitoring, but only during an employee's first few weeks on the job. The result is that deposits into the social bank account are short-lived and employee motivation and enthusiasm begins to wane. Ongoing side-by-side assistance helps you easily correct minor bad habits before they grow into larger concerns. It creates an opportunity to offer genuine, instant positive feedback.

A good rule of thumb is to spend *at least* one half-day, four times a year with each of your customer contact employees. This should be person-to-person, quality time. Be sure to schedule it in advance and make the time sacred.

The most useful feedback is a quantitative measure of each component of the customer interaction. A feedback form is an essential tool in this process. Assign a numerical value for each expected behavior. For example, a perfectly executed greeting might be worth three points. An employee who forgot to offer his name might be awarded only one point. A poor greeting earns no points.

The score for each service component is measured and totaled. In addition to scoring the greeting, you can measure: accessing the account in a customer friendly way, the use of favor language, providing the Johnny Most, and the use of the customer's name during the conversation. At the conclusion of the call, you can share your evaluation with your employee. The numerical values help the employee see improvement from one customer contact to the next. The sample checklist form included here can serve as a model for the form you'll want to create.

CSR Do-right™ ✓ Checklist
© 1990 Steve Broydrick Seminars

Scoring
Exceptional - 3
Yes - 2
No - 0

Phone Greeting Correct?
Ex ☐   Yes ☐   No ☐

Today's Date ____/____/____
Employee's Name ____
What was missing/unnecessary? ____

Scoring Average
2 or better - Rewardable
1 to 2 - Commendable
½ to 1 - Improvable
0 to ½ - Deplorable!

Billing Questions	Ex ✓	Yes ✓	No ✓
Let customer speak			
Pull acct. in friendly way			
Gave "Johnny Most" re: computer			
Used customer's name			
Used "favor" language			
If place "on hold," asked			
Avoided technical jargon			
Showed patience in explaining bill			
Empathized if customer frustrated			
Removed customer's anxiety			
Assumed customer's honesty			
Wrapped up call			
Used name at end of call			
Bonus: Offered Tip for Tonight			
Total Points			

☞ Average

Sales Opportunity	Ex ✓	Yes ✓	No ✓
Let customer speak			
Asked, "Are you familiar with...?"			
Began by learning customer's interests			
Used "favor" language			
Discussed handful, not ALL 14 programs			
Said, "I have it, I like it..."			
Mentioned specific movie programs			
Discussed current promotions			
Led with premium instead of basic			
Assured customer of good decision			
Explained pricing thoroughly			
Wrapped up call			
Used name at end of call			
Bonus: Offered Tip for Tonight			
Total Points			

☞ Average

Outage/Repair	Ex ✓	Yes ✓	No ✓
Let customer speak			
Pulled acct. in friendly way			
Gave "Johnny Most" re: computer			
Used "favor" language			
Used customer's name			
Suggested use phone near TV			
Attempted to solve over-the-phone			
Made good judgement of customer's tech level			
Sold customer on over-the-phone troubleshooting			
If outage, explained in friendly way			
Gave time frame for return to service			
Scheduled necessary repair visit			
Wrapped up call			
Used name at end of call			
Total Points			

☞ Average

Audrey Prior, a former customer service supervisor at Contel of Maine and now GTE's state manager of external affairs, decided excellent performance deserved more than a high score. She gave M&M candies to each representative as an instant reward for a job well done. To Audrey and her staff, the initials M&M stood for "measurable and meaningful."

Shoulder-to-shoulder monitoring leads to natural and relaxed correction of mistakes. Consider these ways to motivate an employee to improve:

• *Lead with praise.* Point out what the employee did that favorably impressed you. She will be more likely to respond favorably to the constructive criticism that follows.[15]

• *Leave the "buts" out.* The sincerity and effectiveness of the opening words of praise are lost if you use the word *but* as the conjunction in a sentence that combines praise and criticism: "John, you have a very pleasant speaking voice *but* you're using too much command language."

Semantically, the word *but* directs the listener to what is said *after* that word. The praise is missed and the listener hears only criticism.

This method would be more effective: "John, you have a very pleasant speaking voice *and* I think I can give you an idea of how to use it even more effectively."

The conjunction "and" tells the listener that both parts of the sentence are of equal importance.[16]

• *Focus on WIIFM behavior.* WIIFM stands for "What's in it for me?" Before attempting to correct a behavior, ask yourself, "What benefit will my employee derive from the behavioral change I'm suggesting?" For example, if you're asking that he use less command language, point out how the change will cause his customers to be more pleasant and cooperative.

Perhaps your present monitoring method is to listen to customer phone calls from a remote location. Your representatives know you'll be listening but never know when the monitoring is taking place. This technique isn't supportive; it's surveillance. Your feedback cannot be instant because you're not with the employee. You'll capture plenty of mistakes but will lack a spontaneous way to correct them.

There are only two situations where remote monitoring is recommended:

• A customer service supervisor points out that shoulder-to-shoulder monitoring isn't effective with every member of her staff. "Certain repretives are model citizens in my presence. I only discover areas that require attention when I conduct remote monitoring."

• Some customer service representatives might prefer remote monitoring because they find shoulder-to-shoulder contact nerve racking. If an employee actually prefers to be monitored remotely, he should be accommodated.

Give Up Your Office

A Federal Express Customer Service Center consists of centrally located managers' workstations that are encircled by clusters of six customer service representatives' work spaces. Each customer service representative has quick and easy access to managers and co-workers for questions and points of clarification.[17]

Federal Express is the exception. Most customer service managers have offices and doors to assure privacy. Rather than easy accessibility, customer service representatives get plenty of exercise walking from their work area to the office. If the manager's door is closed most of the time, they stop making the trip. The silent message is, "You're on your own."

Especially morale deflating is the managerial practice of calling individual employees into an office and closing the door. Other employees begin to speculate and gossip about what's being said. The manager's office is not seen as a place for praise but as a woodshed where employees go to receive their verbal equivalent of 40 lashes.

Federal Express has the right idea. Offices and doors serve as impediments to employee contact. When privacy is required, the supervisor can seek out a conference room or an area away from the work space.

These ideas remove the first obstacle to employee satisfaction: *"I only see or hear from my supervisor when I mess up."* It's almost impossible to provide too much genuine praise. Being readily available and scheduling regular shoulder-to-shoulder feedback will help keep your employees satisfied.

The second obstacle to employee satisfaction is: *"I don't know what's going on around here."* Customer contact employees often tell me they first learn of promotional offers and special sales from their customers rather than their supervisors. When supervisors are questioned about this, they'll remark, "I sent a memo to everyone in the department about the new sales promotion." Just because an employee knows how to read doesn't guarantee she will read. It's critical to hold regularly scheduled, energy-filled, informative employee meetings. There are several types of useful meetings.

All-hands meetings. This is a gathering of all employees in all departments. An all-hands meeting can be used to share the company's upcoming goals and objectives. It's an opportunity to make general announcements, clarify important points, and have some fun. Here are some ideas for an effective all-hands meeting:

• *Hold it first thing in the morning/at the beginning of a shift.* Reach people when they're fresh. Scheduling the meeting at the beginning of the day also ensures the meeting won't be interminable. It creates a natural ending point and an energizing start to the day.

• *Tape it for those who can't attend.* This allows employees who were unable to attend to listen to or watch what was said and done.

• *Begin with an announcement of the date and time of the next meeting.* Give employees plenty of notice. It helps ensure that they schedule other activities around the meeting.

• *Announce birthdays, anniversaries, and births.* It's a great way to recognize individuals in a fun, upbeat way. Find an outgoing employee who has a good singing voice to lead the group in "Happy Birthday to You."

• *Fill it with applause.* Applause is the great energizer. Use it liberally. This meeting is a great place to present awards, read letters of praise from customers, and recognize employees for any and all extraordinary efforts.

One of our clients rewards each employee achievement with a reach into the *grab bag.* The recognized employee comes to the front of the room and reaches into a bag filled with gift certificates from local businesses such as restaurants, movie theaters, and music stores. After selecting the gift certificate, the prize is announced to the rest of the group. It adds a touch of spontaneity to the festivities.

The same company sees to it that all letters of praise from customers are not only read but posted on the wall of the employee break room until the next meeting. They call it the *Wall of Fame.*

• *Read and discuss important memos.* Remember, the written word doesn't guarantee dissemination of important information. Go over each memorandum that was sent to all employees. Field questions and clarify points as necessary.

All-hands meetings are not recommended for organizations facing low morale or lacking a strong leader. When not carefully conducted and orchestrated, they can degenerate into a gripe session. One method to prevent negative comments is to establish the ground rule that no one is permitted to criticize an existing way of doing business without offering an alternative or solution.

Department meetings. These should take place as frequently as possible, at least once a week. Some businesses schedule a meeting every day and before each shift. At Olive Garden Restaurants, wait staff begins the day with an "alley rally." This stand-up meeting includes an announcement of the day's specials and a discussion of current sales goals. It concludes with a motivational thought of the day from one of the wait staff and the singing of the restaurant song.[18] Every day, similar meetings are held at Legal Sea Foods, Inc. Servers learn about and sample the restaurant's specials of the day.

The usefulness of daily meetings isn't limited to restaurants. For example, many dental practices engage in similar preparation. The staff spends about 20 minutes discussing the patients and procedures scheduled during the upcoming workday. Hygienists share insights about expected patients, "Does she have a low tolerance for pain? What are her special interests that I might discuss with her during her visit?"

Where Are We Going?

The third obstacle to employee satisfaction is: *"I see no connection between what I do and how I get rewarded."*

The One Minute Manager is an allegory about a young man in search of management wisdom. One of the stories he hears is of a manager plagued by unmotivated, unenthusiastic employees. One night, the manager goes bowling. He hears an excited commotion a few alleys away. Looking closely, he realizes that the people jumping up and down are the same people he can't seem to motivate at work. "Why are they so excited here and so listless on the job?" The answer to the question helped him change the level of his employees' performance.

At the bowling alley, his people could see success. The more fallen pins, the more successful they were. At work, there were no pins. Employees had no goals or direction.[19]

Can your employees see the pins? What are your department's goals? Have you effectively communicated them to your staff? Are they measured and rewarded? Stop for a moment, put down this book, and write down three goals that have been established for your people. Jot down how you're measuring those goals and what, if any, rewards your people receive for reaching those goals.

One of the best goals for a customer service organization is a quantitative measurement of customer satisfaction. The company can set numerical goals for customer survey results. Using a time line chart, employees can see what trends in customer satisfaction have developed. Sales goals can also be measured and shared with your staff. Each meeting, results can be announced and discussed.

Get graphic. All goals should be measured and displayed on charts, graphs and bulb thermometers. Post your progress in the lunch- or breakroom where employees are sure to see them. Use your graphs during your department or all-hands meetings. Visuals make goals come alive.

My first visit to the breakroom at Stew Leonard's Dairy was an eye-opener. I watched one of the meat department employees enter the room. Instead of heading straight for the vending machines, he approached a wall. There he carefully studied his department's latest survey results. He was more hungry for information than food.

Rewards

Goals can be attained with either carrots or a stick. The implicit stick might be, "Reach this goal or you'll no longer work here." The carrot, "If you meet or exceed this goal, you'll witness greater recognition, appreciation, and a fatter paycheck."

Every employee would love those carrots but employers wonder how to pay for them. The right goals shouldn't cost a company money; they should create higher profits. It's possible to give employees a bigger piece of pie by growing the size of the pie.

For example, let's say you supervise a group of technical assistance representatives. Some of your people answer telephone calls; others make house calls to repair equipment. You know your repair technicians are overworked, and they've told you they prefer free time to overtime. They have so many house calls scheduled that customers are waiting close to a week to be serviced. Furthermore, house calls are expensive. You're paying out too much in overtime, gas, oil, and vehicle maintenance.

The repair techs are also complaining that many of the house calls are unnecessary. "The telephone rep could have solved her problem over the phone. I didn't even need to be there." Your goal is to reduce your overhead, solve customers' problems more quickly, and increase your repair technicians' and telephone representatives' job satisfaction by rewarding them for reducing the company's overhead.

First, you explain to all your employees that 48 percent of last month's phone calls required an in-home service call. You've calculated that a 10 percent decrease in in-home service calls would eliminate a significant piece of overhead, thus saving the department $3,200 a month. You have 16 employees and decide that if the in-home service calls can be reduced to 38 percent of all calls, you'll give half of the savings to your employees. Notice that everybody wins. Profits and paychecks both increase.

You tell your staff that if, in the month of November, the percentage of calls requiring a repair visit is 38 percent or lower, every employee will receive a $100 bonus and that the bonus will continue for the next three months in every month that the goal is reached. You make it clear that the percentage cannot be shaved at the expense of customer satisfaction. There should be no concurrent increase in repeat service calls because the telephone troubleshooting was ineffective.

Your next move is to the breakroom where you ask an artistic employee to draw a giant bulb thermometer that will chart the weekly progress of the group's effort. The goals are discussed at every departmental meeting.

Keep It Fresh

As goals are reached and exceeded, they can be changed or made more challenging. Ask your employees what rewards would motivate them. You might discover more creative and less expensive responses than money. Some departments celebrate with a pizza party or tickets to a concert or a local amusement park. One often-overlooked motivator is time off. It's a satisfying reward that a company purchases at wholesale.

The best goals reward both individual and group achievement. Suppose you worked for a telephone company as a customer service supervisor.

Your company offers a variety of profitable custom calling features like call waiting, call forwarding, and speed dialing. Sales for these services are at an all-time low. Through employee monitoring, you discover why. Your representatives aren't even mentioning them!

With the assistance of your financial people, you calculate what additional profits would be realized by a 10 percent increase in custom calling sales. You receive approval to share the profits with your staff, but instead of establishing only a departmental reward, individual rewards are also included.

Each customer service representative is now expected to sell $50 in custom calling features each month. Once the $50 threshold is reached, a commission equal to the first month's custom calling revenues is paid on all sales above the threshold. Each employee also shares in the rewards of reaching the department's goal. If the department's representatives sell 1,800 custom calling features by year-end, each will receive a $500 bonus. Note that both individual initiative and group effort are being rewarded.

Curing Departmental Sclerosis

The fourth obstacle to employee satisfaction is: *"The customer wants me to untangle his problem, but my hands are tied behind my back."*

We'll call this phenomenon *departmental sclerosis*. It's a hardening of the walls between departments. In this type of organization, each employee has very narrowly defined responsibilities. If the customer's request can't be found in the employee's job description, the customer is sent to another department. It's reminiscent of the way Henry Ford built cars. One person attached the left front tire, a different individual secured the right. Employees learned one skill and had minimal versatility.

One-stop shopping is the antidote for such specialization. The term refers to offering a customer service "supermarket" where one call to one company representative fulfills all of the customer's needs. Employees are cross-trained so they can solve a wider variety of customer problems. The employee's ability to provide direct solutions and transfer fewer calls creates a commensurate increase in job satisfaction. Instead of the customer hearing, "I'll have to transfer you," he now hears, "*I* can help you with that." Responding in the latter fashion speeds service and creates more opportunities for the employee to feel a sense of accomplishment.

American Express's service for its cardmembers is an excellent example of a one-stop shopping operation. Though cardmembers call with an almost infinite variety of questions and requests, one customer service representative is prepared to respond to almost every conceivable customer need. One phone call resolves account balance inquiries, disputed charges, even information on how to contact a family member who's overseas and using an American Express card. When the customer service representative doesn't have the answer, he utilizes the company's quick reference guide to find the person or the department that will have the answer.

A spokesman for American Express explains, "A customer's request may require the involvement of several American Express employees. But our cardmember usually needs to speak to just one individual who can coordinate all of the behind-the-scenes efforts made on the cardmember's behalf."[20]

Cross-training also makes you more adaptable. When phone calls reach an exceptional peak, employees can be switched to the affected area to help handle the surge. A cross-trained staff also helps ensure that moderate absenteeism will not have a deleterious effect on productivity. Employees with a broader scope of abilities can fill in anywhere she is needed.

One-stop shopping can also eliminate the need for an automated response unit (ARU). Once each customer service representative is equipped with a complete array of problem-solving skills, all calls can be sent directly to any available representative.

The other method of untying an employee's hands is to give him more decision-making power. When one-stop shopping is combined with an empowered work force, happier customers are sure to follow. The message that should be constantly drilled into each employee is, "You have the power. Solve the problem yourself." When a customer needs help, she wants to pay *one* visit to the place of business. She wants to make *one* phone call. Many businesses are striving to make the transfer button obsolete, compiling telephone statistics showing over 90 percent of customers' calls completed without a transfer.

Other Morale Boosters

When an employee is recognized by a customer for her exceptional service, she should be recognized by her supervisor. A figurative pat on the back or a quick note delivered to her desk are both fine. But more deliberate and thorough signs of appreciation will motivate the employee to make exceptional service a habit.

The all-hands meeting or department meeting are both excellent forums for public recognition, but according to many frontline employees, private praise is even more meaningful. Tom Sharrard, president of Warner Cable in Milwaukee, takes the time to write a letter to every employee who receives accolades from customers. But instead of dropping the letter on the employee's desk, he mails the letter to the employee at home where it can be more easily shared with family and loved ones.

Roger Nunley of Coca-Cola USA in Atlanta has created a fun way to give each employee some public recognition. He keeps a careful eye on upcoming birthdays in his department. The night before each big day, he ensures that voice mail messages are left for everyone but the person celebrating the birthday. This assures that the slightly older person receives plenty of attention and some good-natured teasing.

Bob Gessner, vice president of Massillon Cable TV in Massillon, Ohio, sends a birthday card home to each of the young children of his employees. Sharrard, Nunley, and Gessner are using creative ideas to give their respective businesses more of a family feeling.

ATTITUDE LEADERSHIP

The most effective supervisors are attitude leaders. Employee morale and disposition accurately reflect the attitude a supervisor presents to employees. Though rarely mentioned in a job description, an effective supervisor knows her efforts to motivate her staff will improve the way her staff deals with customers. How do you become an attitude leader?

• *By learning to laugh at yourself.* Remember the school fairs you attended as a youngster? There was probably a dunking tank where teachers volunteered to sit on a plank and wait until a student threw a ball at a target that caused the plank to release and drop the teacher in the water.

Do you recall the teacher who was the first to volunteer to get wet? It was probably the one you liked the most, the one who didn't take himself too seriously. The teacher you most wanted to soak, the one with the high and mighty attitude, probably stayed at home that night.

Stop and ask yourself, "Which teacher am I in the eyes of my staff—the plank sitter or the house sitter?" People find it much easier to relate to an individual with a ready and self-deprecating sense of humor.

• *By greeting everyone enthusiastically.* Be your employee's wake up call. Tomorrow morning, you can be the first enthusiastic person your employee encounters. Enthusiasm is a healthy and highly contagious social condition.

• *By establishing a problem-free department.* Teach your people to avoid the word *problem* and use the neutral term *situation* in its place. You can say, "Mary Ann, we've got a problem," or, "Mary Ann, I have a situation that's just come to my attention." Using the word problem causes you to dwell on the downside consequences rather than the potential benefits unleashed through creative thinking. Problems tend to remain problems. Situations become opportunities.

Airline pilots use the word *attitude* to describe an aircraft's heading relative to the oncoming horizon. Anyone in an organization who sees a brighter horizon becomes an attitude leader: a supervisor, the senior vice president, or the person just hired in the mail room. One thing is certain: The individual who sits in the cockpit of his own mental airplane and looks up, flies up.

You'll learn how to lift off on a new positive course in our next chapter.

Here are the three ideas from this chapter that I will use right away:

1. _____

2. _____

3. _____

Chapter Nine

Attitude Makes the Difference

Sow a thought, and you reap an act;
Sow an act, and you reap a habit;
Sow a habit, and you reap a character;
Sow a character, and you reap a destiny.

Anonymous
Quoted by Samuel Smiles, 1887

Two people sit three desks apart. They deal with the same customers. One loves her job; the other anxiously awaits the weekend. Two people look at the same sky but announce totally different forecasts. One sees partly sunny, the other partly cloudy. Two people reach their 40th birthdays; one throws a big party, while the other goes into mourning. Is it really the beginning of the end or just the end of the beginning?

Your attitude makes the difference. The person who arrives at work with positive expectations gets what she expects. So does the individual who anticipates dealing with an endless string of difficult customers. Customers provide us with a mirror, which produces an image vivid and true. Expect the best from those you serve and they will reflect your desire to give them your very best.

Your attitude is the outward reflection of your thoughts. Your thoughts are just about everything. Marcus Aurelius said, "Our life is what our thoughts make it." Abraham Lincoln once remarked, "I believe that a man is about as happy as he makes up his mind to be." British essayist James Allen wrote, "A man is literally what he thinks, his character being the complete sum of his thoughts."[1] Contemporary psychologist Martin E. P. Seligman says, "Our thoughts are not merely reactions to events; they change what ensues."[2]

126

Focused thinking is one of the most powerful forces on earth. Each of us has the ability to choose our thoughts and our response to every person, event, or circumstance. If you're unwilling to make the choice, your thoughts will be random, negative, and enervating. Thoughts have life-changing power, not when they are knee-jerk reactions to situations but when they are carefully selected. Through this process, your mind is transformed from dictatorship to democracy.

One transformed person begins to influence the attitudes of others. Perhaps you've observed with some amazement as one positive person enters an office and changes the entire atmosphere of the space. You can have a similar impact in your workplace. It requires a commitment to become an attitude leader. If you don't make a conscious, courageous decision to influence, you will be influenced.

CHARACTERISTICS OF ATTITUDE LEADERS

Those people who say yes to the challenges of the workplace are the ones who prepare for the workday and go the extra mental mile. Like a dedicated athlete, they develop work habits and don't quit at the first sign of adversity.

A sense of satisfaction comes not from the easy days, but from sticking with it when extra effort is required. Having the opportunity to observe and work with Olympic-caliber customer service professionals, let me offer the characteristics they share in common:

• *They are physically active.* They get regular physical exercise. Stop by the office at lunch and you won't find them. They're probably outside taking a brisk walk. They use this safe productive method to burn off any morning stress and to recharge for the challenges of the afternoon.

• *They are spiritually grounded.* Though their belief systems vary widely, they take their service role seriously, feeling that all customers deserve to be treated with respect. They practice the second commandment, "Love thy neighbor," in the way they treat both customers and co-workers.

• *They are mentally tough.* Many have lived through personal hardships and have emerged wiser, stronger, and determined to successfully overcome any future crises or setbacks.

• *They're less interested in what people think.* They focus on what their energy and enthusiasm can make other people feel.

• *They mentally prepare for every workday.* These are not the jump out of bed, jump in the shower, jump in the car types. They take the time to slowly and gradually loosen up the muscle between the ears.

BECOMING AN ATTITUDE LEADER

Here are the three steps you can take to join the ranks of the attitude leaders:

• Paint your day.
• Draw a map.
• Act enthusiastically.

Paint Your Day

Ask your co-workers, "What happens before you even get to work to make you think it's going to be a bad day?" The response you'll hear most frequently is, "When I oversleep and wake up late." Employees say that if they wake up late they feel that the day controls them rather than feeling that they control the day.

The single best way to improve your daily performance is to wake up 20 minutes earlier and prepare for it. A pitcher for a major league baseball team doesn't show up five minutes before game time. He doesn't walk out to the mound and start hurling the ball at 93 miles an hour. He arrives early, stretches his muscles, jogs around the outfield, and then begins to throw the ball easily in the bullpen until his arm is warmed up.

A professional dancer doesn't walk into a recital hall and immediately attempt amazing leaps and gravity-defying maneuvers. She slowly, gradually holds her muscles at a mild angle of tension so they can be extended and warmed up. The difference between an amateur and a professional is that the professional is willing to take the time to prepare before the audience, the fans, or the customers arrive. The amateur pushes the snooze button.

Getting up early is not easy. By arising 20 minutes earlier, you may be fighting your internal biological clock. Researchers now understand that most people don't operate on a natural 24 hour cycle. This sleepability-wakeability rhythm is often 25 hours in length.[3] For some people, each day is like switching back to daylight savings time. This makes it easier for most people to go to bed a little later each night and wake up a little later each morning.

Perhaps this helps explain why you often find yourself running behind schedule in the morning. You've created conditions by which you're at the mercy of people, events, and circumstances. Thoughts and responses are no longer chosen, but reflexive. You grow angry and frustrated at the dresser for lacking clean clothes or the refrigerator for not going to the market and buying some milk. Later as you drive to work, you discover that everyone on the road but you needs driving lessons.

Only through early morning mental preparation do you gain control. All the thoughts of the day can be chosen through the slow and gradual preparation of your mind during these 20 minutes. The foundation for a positive attitude can only be created by fighting the biological tug to roll over. You must decide which will do you more good—20 minutes or 40 winks.

Mental breakfast. Find the spot in your house or apartment that is quiet and has a good reading light. Spend the first 10 minutes or so reading something that's positive, motivational, or inspirational. Your mind awakens before your body. It's hungry, empty, and receptive to anything you choose to feed it. Each morning begins with a *mental breakfast*. Until now, your menu selection may not have been beneficial.

Your current habit may be to awaken to a clock radio that announces various overnight tragedies. You might then turn on the television and receive a broader scope of murder and mayhem. The next step might be to read similar reports in your morning newspaper. Are you on your way to making it a good day?

Psychologists know that good and bad moods can be induced. You have the ability to both create and select from the menu of mental breakfasts. Imagine you wake up tomorrow, turn on the reading lamp, and read the following:

I don't seem to be quite myself today.

In fact, I'm feeling a little low.

My work isn't really going as well as it could.

I'm feeling a little discouraged about it.

In fact, you could say that I'm sort of blue today.

It's hard to see how things are going to get better.

In fact, if anything, they'll probably get worse.

I'm really down today.

I'm feeling so discouraged.

There doesn't seem to be much hope.[4]

This hardly seems the best way to prepare for good performance at work. But these gradually worsening statements impact on your attitude no differently than a morning ritual of all-news radio, television, and the metro section of the newspaper.

Try a more nutritional mental breakfast:

I'm feeling pretty good today.

Things have been going quite well for me.

I think today will be a good day for me.

I've been able to accomplish a lot lately.

I'm feeling quite happy about myself.

My work is really going well.

I think if I put my mind to it, that I can do just about anything.

In fact, I'm feeling really great right now.[5]

Inspirational sections of bookstores are filled with life-affirming mental breakfasts that, unlike your daily newspaper, have stood the test of time. If your budget is tight, use your local library to feed your mind. Some of our clients have begun an office library of motivational books and audio tapes. Employees are free to check out and benefit from these resources.

Paint a picture. The next step of your preparation is to close your book, turn off your reading lamp, close your eyes, and *"paint your day."* Utilizing a mental paintbrush, vividly imagine the events of a productive workday. See the smiles of your co-workers, and hear the thank you of customers and the healthy laughter in the breakroom or cafeteria. Imagine yourself resolving the problem of a difficult customer with poise and confidence. You cannot predict every event of the day, but by mentally rehearsing a professional response, you increase your chances of behaving like a professional during your performance.

Athletes have successfully used this mental visualization technique for years. If you watch Olympic athletes carefully, you'll notice that many perform their routine twice—once in their minds, and a second time with their bodies.

Dwight Stones, the American high jumper, developed a unique rehearsal method. Just prior to each jump, he would stand still and lightly bob his head as he imagined each step towards the bar. You could then watch as his head would swoop from left to right as he saw himself successfully passing over the bar and landing in the pit area. Only after this mental jump did he attempt a physical one. This technique worked well for Dwight Stones. He won the Olympic Gold Medal for the high jump in 1984.

Jim Thorpe, one the greatest of all 20th-century athletes, also knew the value of seeing a great performance. Thorpe was once on his way to Europe by ship to compete in the Olympics. Most athletes worked out furiously on the ship's deck, running, jumping, and lifting weights. One of the coaches came upon Thorpe sitting on the deck, leaning against a lifeboat, eyes closed, not even in his track suit. "Thorpe," he said sharply, "what do you think you're doing?" The big, bronzed athlete opened one eye and said, "I'm watching myself win the decathlon."[6]

Meditation can also be practiced in the early morning. For centuries, people of diverse cultures have experienced serenity and an improved sense of well-being from this oasis in a busy day. The relaxation response, mentioned in the chapter on irate customers, embodies the latest medical thinking on meditative technique. Here's a review of its basic steps:

- Pick a focus word or short phrase that's firmly rooted in your personal belief system.
- Sit quietly in a comfortable position.
- Close your eyes.
- Relax your muscles.
- Breath slowly and naturally.
- Assume a passive attitude. Don't worry how you're doing.
- Continue for 10 or 20 minutes.
- Practice once or twice daily.[7]

Other attitude leaders choose prayer because it helps fortify their spiritual roots. Spending this early morning time well provides you with a greater sense of control over the day.

In *Gift From the Sea*, Anne Morrow Lindbergh shares a lesson too easily forgotten. Reflecting on a moon shell in front of her, she writes: "You will remind me that I must try to be alone for part of each year, even a week or a few days; and for a part of each day, even for an hour or a few minutes in order to keep my core, my center, my island quality."[8]

Draw a Map

The best way to a successful day is to create a plan for each workday and then mentally focus on that plan. Time management courses advocate preparing a to-do list because it helps ensure that important tasks are accomplished. But having a plan does more than simply guarantee productivity. It helps you maintain a positive attitude. Knowing that your attitude is the outward reflection of your thoughts, consider these characteristics of thoughts:

- Your mind can only hold one thought at a time.
- Positive thoughts and emotions live in today; negative thoughts and emotions live elsewhere.

Your mind never takes a day off. Thoughts are constantly created and brought to the surface. Useful, productive work helps create thoughts that are focused, orderly, and directed. When your mind is totally engaged in accomplishing today's tasks, it becomes impossible to engage in *mental time travel*. Without total focus on today, your mind either drifts into the past or the future, entering places over which it has no control or influence. The past is unchangeable. The future is controllable only to the degree you focus on accomplishing useful tasks today.

When your mind travels to the past, it may do more than conjure pleasant memories. Perhaps you recall some of your all-time major blunders, wishing now that you had made different choices. You're removing positive thoughts of today and replacing them with negative thoughts of yesterday. The day's positive momentum has been interrupted.

The other dangerous locale is the future. With blurred predictive vision, you may spin out endless fantasies of doom and gloom. What we can't see or can't know causes many of us to expect the worst. Today's positive thoughts and tomorrow's awfulizing cannot coexist.[9] One or the other will win out.

In his book, *Flow: The Psychology of Optimal Experience*, Mihalyi Csikszentmihalyi describes the ideal conditions for negative thought:

> with nothing to do, the mind is unable to prevent negative thoughts from elbowing their way to center stage. . . . Worries about one's love life, health, investments, family and job are always hovering at the periphery of attention waiting until there is nothing pressing that demands concentration. As soon as the mind is ready to relax, zap! the potential problems that were waiting in the wings take over.[10]

It is possible to worry about absolutely everything and anything. Suppose you receive a message to call your spouse. When you attempt the call, the line is busy. Your mind might immediately shift into overdrive, imagining some unexpected family or personal emergency.

What if you discover a message on your desk from your supervisor. It simply says "Please see me first thing tomorrow morning." You may begin to read between the lines. Will tomorrow be your final day working for your present employer? Like a spider creating her web, your mind begins to spin the countless negative consequences of tomorrow's unexpected meeting.

You have no control over what will happen tomorrow. Focusing on the unknown is a tempting but unproductive use of brain power. The best protection from this mental drift is to *draw a map*. Like a ship's navigator, you can focus on a single purpose—the successful completion of passage to the end of the day.

Only when your plans are realistic do you reinforce a positive attitude. Beware of composing a to-do list with more items than could possibly be accomplished in a single day. You'll dwell more on what you didn't accomplish than what you did. Your objective should be to reach the end of the day with your task list fully completed.

In his book, *The Greatest Salesman in the World Part II—The End of the Story*, Og Mandino writes, "Now I know the wise man never makes goals of immense proportions. Those plans that are giant in size he cradles them close to his heart where others may not see or mock. Then he greets the morning with goals for the day only and he makes certain that all he has planned is completed before he sleeps."[11]

My father once sold a paint called Drylok®, which, when applied to basement walls, protected the home's foundation from water damage. Think of your daily map as "Drylok for the brain." Negative thoughts find it impossible to penetrate the walls of a well-planned day.

Act Enthusiastically

You've invested 20 minutes in daily preparation. You have a plan for the day. It's show time. Act enthusiastically! Your co-workers and customers need it. Chances are they haven't made similar mental preparation but are poised to respond to your attitude. Customers and co-workers tend to behave like attitude chameleons, taking on the color of the emotions you send their way.

The power of positive emotions. Medical and psychological researchers now understand that positive emotions pay dividends. Laughter, hope, and enthusiasm benefit you—the expressor—as well as those around you—the receivers.

In her book, *Positive Illusions*, psychologist Shelley Taylor argues that seeing life through slightly rose-colored glasses helps us better cope with our trials and tribulations and that holding a hopeful view of the present and future is an indicator of sound mental health.[12]

In the late 1970s, neuroscientist Karen Bulloch traced direct neurological pathways between the brain and the immune system.[13] Medical research quickly entered a new and exciting field, studying the interconnections between psychological and emotional states and the body's nervous, endocrine, and immune systems. Known as psychoneuroimmunology (PNI), researchers are discovering links between positive emotions and physical well-being. Studies indicate that both the *expression* and *reception* of emotions appear to strengthen the body's immune function.

In research conducted at Stanford University and the University of California at Berkeley, severely ill cancer patients were divided into two groups. One group participated in support meetings that gave them a chance to express feelings about their condition as well as feel the bond of socialization. The second or control group experienced no such intervention. Those in the intervention group lived on average 18 months longer than those in the control group.[14]

Another study used a similar approach with less severely ill cancer patients. A full six months after social and psychiatric intervention was completed, the intervention group continued to show significantly higher levels of certain immune cells.[15]

Expression of positive emotions might also work with nature towards improving our health. In a study at the University of California, Los Angeles, a group of actors was asked to present a series of brief performances. Their task was to improvise a monologue that would elicit either happy or sad emotions. After each performance, the actors' blood chemistry was measured. After expressing intense joy, laughter, and hope, higher levels of natural killer (NK) immune cells were found.[16]

Hearing this good news, you would expect your co-workers to become more positive people. If people know that attitude makes the difference, why don't more people have a different attitude? Because being positive is hard work. Negative mental habits are easier than positive mental habits. Fear is easier than faith. Resentment is easier than forgiveness. Criticism is easier than praise. Cynicism is easier than enthusiasm.

There always seems to be someone ready to burst your balloon of enthusiasm. Tell certain people you're getting married and they'll say, "That is the biggest mistake you'll ever make. Are you sure you've thought this through? I hope yours works out better than mine did!"

Tell the cynic you're expecting your first child and he'll remark, "Your life will never be the same." It takes mental exertion to retain your joy and cast his comments aside. One of the reasons expressing enthusiasm is so challenging is that most people are not enthusiastic.[17]

Bringing out enthusiasm. The new manager of a banquet center was surprised when she first began taking phone calls to book wedding receptions. Young women would call and in sheepish voices say, "Hello, my fiance and I are getting married next June and we're looking for a place to have our reception." The banquet manager said some of these women sounded almost apologetic they were getting married. Chances are they were once enthusiastic about their impending matrimony until certain friends and family members began launching their grenades of cynicism.

The banquet manager decided she had heard enough. "This is not the attitude to express about the most joyous day of your life," she thought. She decided to become an attitude leader. When the phone rings and the young woman on the other end begins to meekly describe her upcoming wedding, the banquet manager exclaims, "You're getting married? That's fantastic! We'd love to be part of your big day."

The change is sudden and predictable. The bride-to-be catches the banquet manager's bouquet of enthusiasm and begins to speak with energy about her wedding plans. The banquet manager draws out the young woman's natural inclination towards enthusiasm.

Go out on a limb. Our seminar attendees are often asked, "What would happen if you walked into your office tomorrow and in a big enthusiastic voice said, "Today's going to be a great day!" How would your co-workers react? The answers include, "They would think I had lost my marbles." "They would figure I was putting on some kind of act." "They'd think I was some kind of phoney." But think back to the characteristics of the attitude leader. They could care less what people think, caring more about what people feel. Remember, expression and reception of positive emotions do your body, mind, and soul some good.

The reason more people don't walk into work each day and express enthusiasm is because expressing enthusiasm is a social risk. One of the deepest cravings of every person is to be accepted by others. Acceptance comes more easily from a negative or cynical remark and is the path of least resistance. With a choice between hard work and easy acceptance, acceptance usually wins.

Make that enthusiastic comment and you find yourself out on a limb. If the branch breaks, you face possible isolation or embarrassment. But the only way to see what a difference one positive attitude can make is to take the risk. You'll reap the reward.

Over the years, I've watched people climb out on that limb and turn on the lights in their workplace—people like Anderson Hughes, the silver-haired bellman at the Detroit Airport Marriott who, with childlike enthusiasm, reminds his early morning guests what a good day it's going to be. Or the flight attendant I encountered one day on a rickety commuter plane traveling from Minneapolis to Duluth. With boundless energy and great wit, she reassured even the most jittery passengers that we would arrive in one piece.

Or Wally Olson driving the Number 8 bus in Santa Monica, who decided years ago to put his heart, soul, and singing voice into his job. On the rainy January afternoon I met him, he was serenading his passengers with "Pennies from Heaven," "You Are My Sunshine," and "April Showers." It was dark and dreary outside, but Wally had discovered the secret of creating his own weather.[18]

These individuals may seem special but they're really no different than you and me. They just get up each morning and recommit to climbing out on that limb. They recognize that without the risk of enthusiasm there can be no reward. If you asked them for advice, what would they tell you?

Throw yourself into your work. Autograph it with your personality. That, my friend, makes all the difference.

Here are the three ideas from this chapter that I will use right away:

1. _____

2. _____

3. _____

Appendix

Door-to-Door Service

D elivering service to a customer's home is one of your company's greatest challenges. Upon crossing the threshold, you enter a world of dogs, cats, and active children. The job requires a host of skills, only one of which is solving the customer's problem. As Walter Coleman of Whirlpool Corporation points out, "The service person has two items to repair—the appliance and the company's reputation."[1]

The professional service person arrives at the door with more than technical skills. He or she also possesses strong people skills. The customer may expect a visit from a company but finds her expectations pleasantly exceeded when she's visited by a personable human being. This blending of people skills and technical skills is the secret to creating a positive impression.

The service person with strong technical skills and weak people skills leaves no better than a neutral impression. He may solve the customer's problem but complete his work in total silence. Under these circumstances, the customer's home feels like an elevator in a high-rise building. Two strangers ride past floor after floor without sharing a word. Both are anxious to arrive at their respective destinations so the discomfort can be alleviated. Remember, it is not the customer's job to make you feel comfortable. It's your responsibility to create rapport.

The service person with wonderful people skills and weak technical skills leaves a negative impression. You may have been voted "most congenial" in your high school graduating class but it's a wasted talent unless it's combined with the ability to satisfactorily resolve the customer's problem.

Here are techniques you can use to ensure that your customer is impressed from the moment you arrive to the time you say goodbye.

START AT THE DOOR

The first time the customer should see you is at his door. Avoid the temptation to first check equipment outside the customer's house. It's disconcerting for a homeowner to look out his window and see a stranger walking through his backyard or investigating the side of his house. Go to the door first, introduce yourself, and explain what you'll be doing outside. Long-distance first impressions are rarely good ones.

The quality of your greeting is not determined solely by what you say but also by how you look. Do you appear to be a professional or someone who just returned from a Hell's Angels convention? Consider these ways to ensure a professional appearance:

Wear your uniform. This is the first of three forms of identification that reassures a customer you are a representative of your company. Your customer feels comfortable allowing you into the house when you're wearing a uniform and driving a vehicle that clearly state the name of your company *and* when you're wearing picture identification. Shady characters occasionally pose as service representatives and violate a homeowner's trust. You remove any sense of misgiving when you can be unquestionably identified as a company representative.

Either have a beard/moustache or don't. Some service organizations have a policy against beards and moustaches. They feel that the best impression is made by a clean-shaven face and that permitting facial hair opens a pandora's box of appearance problems.

Some men will keep their beards or moustaches neatly trimmed; other men will look like they threw away their razors years ago. Some men habitually wear two to three days' worth of beard growth. This may be intended as a fashion statement but many older or conservative customers perceive this "look" as scraggly and unprofessional. If your company permits facial hair, keep it full but neatly trimmed at all times.

Use these ideas to maintain the appearance of your customer's home.

The cable shuffle. A cable television technician in Virginia makes a habit of wiping his feet before entering a customer's home. What's unique about his method is that he *waits until the customer arrives* at the door before shuffling his feet. The customer is made aware of his effort to keep floors and rugs clean.

Check and Show. Another cable television technician in Michigan exhibits her concern in another way. Just before she enters the customer's home, she lifts her foot, grabs it with her hand, and turns the sole of her boot so it's facing the customer while saying, "I just want to show you that my boots are clean before I come in." When used in combination, the cable shuffle and the check and show make a great first impression.

Some customers insist that a service representative remove her boots before entering the home. Some service representatives are unwilling to fulfill this request citing the safety hazard of working in stocking feet. There is a happy medium. The service representative can carry and wear disposable boots. These slip over the boot and protect the customer's floors from outside dirt, snow, rain, or mud. The service representative can work safely and the customer's floors can be protected. Make sure that the disposable boots you purchase provide excellent traction, otherwise you're substituting one work hazard for another.

Arrive equipped to protect the customer's floor and rugs. Asking the customer to lay down newspapers or shopping bags in the employee's path is an unfair imposition. Refusing to remove your boots and insisting that your customer protect his own floors is sure to leave a negative impression.

Provide a friendly greeting. Introduce yourself by name and make a smooth transition to the reason for your visit: "Hi, I'm Mike from the phone company. How can I help you today?" "Good morning, my name is Shirley from the cable company. I'm here to fix your problem." Both greetings express confidence and a can-do attitude. Using your name at the door immediately transforms you from company representative to a fellow human being.

A service technician from Ohio once wrote to me and said, "Using my first name at the door is one of the most useful ideas I've ever learned. It used to be that if I was in one room and the customer was in another, she would yell, 'Hey cable man, I have a question.' Now I hear, 'Hey, Mike, let me ask you a question.' It's more comfortable for both me and the customer."

Offer to go to a side door. Many customers would prefer that you enter the home from the kitchen or garage door. The front door may be rarely used and adjoins the most expensive flooring in the house. As a technical dispatcher once remarked, "It's a lot easier to clean a kitchen floor than a living room rug."

Ask for symptoms, then diagnose. Like a good doctor, you should make the effort to fully understand the customer's problem before you attempt to solve it. The customer is probably anxious to describe what she's experienced. Her information is vital to fully understanding how you should approach a resolution. The service representative unwilling to invest a few minutes in listening is less likely to satisfy the customer and more likely to head down the wrong path trying to solve the problem.

Ask the customer to remove fragile items. Many homes are filled with collectibles, dolls, china, and other meaningful items that may be near your intended work space. If you break the item, you might also break the customer's heart. Play it safe. Ask the customer to do the handling.

Give'em the Johnny Most. Johnny Most, the late Boston Celtics announcer, was first mentioned in the chapter on being friendly. Provide the customer with a brief description of what you're going to do. Asking questions and providing some play-by-play commentary helps break the silence and creates a sense of rapport. Make sure that each trip out of the house is preceded by an announcement of where you're going and when you'll be back. Leave the work space in the condition you found it. We recently had a new telephone line installed. The telephone person left a souvenir of her work—a pile of plaster dust where she had drilled a hole. This is not the best way to be remembered. Many companies now supply each of their service people with a hand-held vacuum cleaner for quick pickups. If your work requires that you move household articles to reach the item requiring servicing, make sure you return these items to their original location.

Are there any other questions I can answer for you today? Make sure the customer fully understands what you've done and is totally satisfied with you and your company. Perhaps the customer recently received a confusing bill from your company and asks you if you can help explain it. You have three ways of handling the request:

1. You can tell the customer he'll have to call the billing department.
2. If you understand your company's billing procedures, you can eliminate any confusion before you leave the premises.
3. You can ask to borrow the customer's phone and call the billing department. This gives the customer immediate access to an individual who can help.

Option number one is the "It's not my job" philosophy. Confronted with such an employee attitude, the customer is tempted to bypass your billing department and instead call your competition. Option number two creates instant satisfaction and promotes customer loyalty. Option three is the next best thing. The customer should be in the process of having her situation resolved before you leave the house.

The service employee who is made aware of a customer's problem should take ownership for the customer's problem until the customer owns a solution.

If the key to creating happy customers could be boiled down to the fewest possible words, they would be:

- Solve the problem yourself.
- Solve the problem the first time.

A customer expects that the service person who appears at her door will be the person who can solve her service problem. To say, "This problem is over my head. We'll have to send someone else out to fix this," begs the question, "Why didn't you send that 'someone else' out here in the first place?"

Offer a business card or company phone number. Many progressive service companies are making sure that customers know where to call should future needs arise. Consider placing your phone number on or near the device you've just serviced. It saves the customer a trip to the phone book and increases the odds that you receive any future business.

Shake hands. Nothing seals a positive impression like hand-to-hand contact. A handshake is most effective at the conclusion of recovery situations where you've transformed a customer from "irateful" to grateful.

Drive carefully. All of your efforts can be wiped out if you wipe out the customer's row of shrubs as you make your getaway! Always do a full 360-degree walk around your truck before you exit. Dogs, cats, and kids are attracted to your vehicle.

DOGS, KIDS, AND SOCIALIZERS

Service technicians often ask, "How do I tactfully deal with the customer who tells me her dog won't bite when the dog's looking at me like he's planning to have me for dinner?" You can politely ask that the dog be put in a room other than where you'll be working. Almost all customers will honor this request if you:

- Are wearing a company uniform.
- Are driving a marked/signed vehicle.
- Can present the customer with picture identification.

Place yourself for a moment in the position of the customer. How would you feel if an unidentifiable person visited your house and asked someone you love to put the family dog away? I'm sure you would want that service person to verify that he was who he said he was.

Make sure the customer understands the reason for your request. Let the customer know that you have been bitten in the past. If the customer refuses to put the dog away, go to your truck, radio the office, and ask the office to call the customer making the same request. If you encounter that rare customer who still refuses to put the dog away, you have the right, in my opinion, to refuse to perform your duties. Once bitten, many service representatives refuse to tempt fate again. Such behavior is both understandable and justified. Make sure you explain the reason the job was left incomplete on the work order.

Kids make service work an adventure. Tools and work orders can disappear. You might have your attention split between the task at hand and countless introductions to real toys or imaginary friends. Children want your attention. They also want to feel important. The solution for outgoing children is to safely channel a child's energy to make him feel important while you get the job done.

Make the child your assistant. Can he be stationed in another room and be given the assignment to let you know when the lights or television or telephone work once again? Your personal space will be reclaimed. A cable television technician in Lebanon, Pennsylvania, offers this suggestion to safely put your little assistant to work. First, ask to borrow the household flashlight. Next, tell the child you need her help: "I need to have you hold this flashlight at just this angle so I can see while I do my work." The service technician said that kids love this new-found sense of responsibility and importance.

The Junior Tech Sticker

The customer remembers the last thing you say or do. One of our clients seals a positive last impression with both children and parents by leaving each child with a sticker. It has the company's name, the words "Junior Technician" printed at the top, and a space to write the child's name. It's a tremendous investment in future goodwill.

How Can I Say Goodbye?

There is one other unique challenge to visiting some customers' homes—exiting gracefully. The older customer who lives alone may enjoy having some much needed company. Unfortunately, you can't stay all day. It wouldn't be fair to other customers who have been promised service that same day. What's the best way to break off a visit without bruising or belittling social needs?

Be honest. Stress fairness to others. "Mrs. Johnson, I've enjoyed talking to you. I really should go. I have five other customers who expect to see me between now and 5 PM. I'm sure you wouldn't want me to let them down." Most customers who have lived more years than you will appreciate your sense of responsibility and commitment to performing your job well.

If you asked customers, "What three attributes in a service person make you anxious to use his company's services again?" this is what you would hear:

- He fixed my problem. (Nothing takes the place of technical competence.)
- He kept my rugs and floors clean.
- She kept me posted. She let me know what she was doing and when she was leaving.

These three items can serve as a mental checklist. Each time you fulfill these customer requirements, you'll know the impression you've created is a positive one.

Here are the three ideas from this appendix that I will use right away:

1. _____

2. _____

3. _____

Notes

Preface

1. Jack Eckerd and Charles Paul Conn, *Finding the Right Prescription* (Old Tappan, N.J.: Fleming H. Revell Company, 1987), pp. 43-44.

Chapter One

1. "Study reveals just how much time is wasted," *Boston Globe*, June 21, 1988.
2. Cavett Robert, keynote speech, opening session, New England Speakers Association, Natick, Mass., March 1990.
3. Richard Larson, telephone interview, August 31, 1990.
4. Richard Larson, "There's More to a Line than Its Wait," *Technology Review*, July 1988, pp. 60+.
5. Douglas M. Ivester, "The Value of Exceeding Consumer Expectations," address, Society of Consumer Affairs Professionals in Business, Atlanta, Ga, April 27, 1992.
6. "Stress on the Job," Newsweek, April 25,1988, pp. 40-45.
7. "How to Motivate Workers: Don't Watch 'em," *Business Week*, April 29, 1991, p. 56.

Chapter Two

1. Maria A. Eksuzian, personal interview, January 6, 1993.
2. Sam Walton with John Huey, *Sam Walton Made in America—My Story* (Garden City, N.Y.: Doubleday Publishing 1992), p. 229.
3. Diane Lewis, telephone interview, December 11, 1992.
4. Tom Peters, "Ode to the Leslies," *Costco Connection* 6, no. 3 (March 1992), p. 5.
5. Cathy McKee, observed during preparation for a seminar, January 1992.
6. Pat Scorpio, observed during preparation for a seminar, 1987.
7. Quoted in "The Profession of Speaking," Joel Weldon, audiotape (Phoenix, Ariz.: National Speakers Association Convention, 1988).
8. I first learned of this idea in a discussion with one of my seminar attendees who had also attended the AT&T program.

Chapter Three

1. Peter Daigle, telephone interview, November 28, 1992.
2. Olof Arnheim, telephone interview, November 23, 1992.
3. Linda Barry, telephone interview, November 23, 1992.

Chapter Four

1. Walter B. Cannon, *Bodily Changes in Pain, Hunger, Fear and Rage* (Boston: Charles T. Branford Company, 1911), 2nd ed. 1953, p. 193.
2. Arlie Russell Hochschild, *The Managed Heart—Commercialization of Human Feeling* (Berkeley: University of California Press, 1983), p. 7.
3. Anne-Marie Eugley, observed during preparation for a seminar, July 1992.
4. Carol Tavris, *Anger—The Misunderstood Emotion* (New York: Simon & Schuster, 1982), p. 132.
5. Walter B. Cannon, *Journal of the American Medical Association* IVI (1911), p. 724.
6. Herbert Benson with William Proctor, *Your Maximum Mind* (New York: Random House, 1987), p. 36.
7. Ibid., pp. 22, 23.
8. Ibid., pp. 169, 179.
9. Tom Peters and Nancy Austin, *A Passion for Excellence* (New York: Random House, 1985), pp. 42-44.

Chapter Five

1. Margaret Prager, telephone interview, January 8, 1993.
2. Marriott representative, telephone interview, October 22, 1993.
3. Chuck Gumushian, telephone interview, October 26, 1993.
4. "Barbie will amend her dumb-blonde response," wire services, *Portland (ME) Press Herald*, October 18, 1992.
5. Stew Leonard, Jr., material provided in response to a telephone request on October, 30, 1992.
6. Walter Coleman, telephone interview, October 30, 1992.
7. William Waers, telephone interview, October 22, 1992.
8. Roger Nunley, telephone interview, October 22, 1992.
9. Christopher W. L. Hart, James L. Heskett, and W. Earl Sasser, "The Profitable Art of Service Recovery," *Harvard Business Review*, July-August 1990, p. 153.
10. David Harris, personal interview, October 17, 1992.
11. Bill Betts, telephone interview, October 29, 1992.
12. James B. Treece, "Getting Mileage from a Recall," *Business Week*, May 25, 1991.

13. Hart et al., "The Profitable Art," p. 149.
14. Peter C. Reid, *Well Made in America—Lessons From Harley-Davidson on Being the Best* (New York: McGraw-Hill, 1990), p. 5.
15. Ibid., p. 30.
16. Ibid., photograph caption, no page.
17. Ibid., p. 91-92.

Chapter Six

1. Carl Rogers, "Barriers and Gateways to Communication," *Harvard Business Review*, November-December 1991, pp. 105-7. Originally published July-August 1952.
2. Stephen R. Covey, *The Seven Habits of Highly Effective People* (New York: Simon & Schuster, 1989), p. 235+.
3. Rogers, "Barriers and Gateways," p. 106.

Chapter Seven

1. Earl Nightingale, "A Worthy Destination," *The New Lead the Field*, audio tape, Nightingale-Conant Corporation, 116-A, n.d.
2. Judy Giordano, observed during preparation for a seminar, March 1990.

Chapter Eight

1. Jill Tavello, telephone interview, January 5, 1993.
2. Bill Waers, telephone interview, January 8, 1993.
3. Walter Coleman, telephone interview, January 12, 1993.
4. Ibid.
5. For a thorough and excellent discussion of customers' ever-changing expectations, see *Total Customer Service—The Ultimate Weapon*, by William H. Davidow and Bro Uttal (New York: Harper & Row, 1989).
6. Roger Nunley, telephone interview, January 8, 1993.
7. Bill Waers, telephone interview, January 8, 1993.
8. Margaret Prager, telephone interview, January 8, 1993.
9. Leonard A. Schlesinger and James L. Heskett, "Customer Satisfaction is Rooted in Employee Satisfaction," *Harvard Business Review*, November-December 1991, p. 148.
10. Ibid., p. 149.
11. Quoted in *How to Win Friends and Influence People*, by Dale Carnegie, 1936. Rev. ed. (New York: Simon & Schuster, 1981), p. 19.
12. Lewis Ephraim, "Confidence in Unions is Crumbling," Business Week, July 8, 1985, p. 76.

13. Hanoch McCarty quoted in "Winning Criticism," by Robert McCarvey, *US Air Magazine*, October 1989, p. 28.
14. Covey, *The Seven Habits*, p. 188+.
15. For more information on the value of praising before criticizing, read the chapter "A Drop of Honey," in Carnegie's *How to Win Friends and Influence People*.
16. Hendrie Weisinger, *The Critical Edge* (New York: Harper & Row, 1990), pp. 61-62.
17. Sherri Strickler, telephone interview, January 8, 1993.
18. Kevin Raymond, telephone interview, January 15, 1993.
19. Kenneth Blanchard and Spencer Johnson, *The One Minute Manager* (New York: William Morrow, 1982), pp. 65-66.
20. American Express, telephone interview, January 28, 1993.

Chapter Nine

1. James Allen, *As a Man Thinketh* (Mount Vernon, N.Y.: Peter Pauper Press, n.d.), p. 7.
2. Martin E. P. Seligman, *Learned Optimism* (New York: Alfred A. Knopf, 1991), p. 7.
3. Jeremy Campbell, *Winston Churchill's Afternoon Nap* (New York: Simon & Schuster, 1986), pp. 195-96.
4. Shelley E. Taylor, *Positive Illusions—Creative Self-Deception and the Healthy Mind* (New York: Basic Books, [a division of HarperCollins Publishers] 1989), p. 51.
5. Ibid., pp. 51-52.
6. Quoted in *Dynamic Imaging* by Norman Vincent Peale (Old Tappan, N.J.: Fleming H. Revell Company, 1982), pp. 153-54.
7. Herbert Benson with William Proctor, *Your Maximum Mind* (New York: Random House, 1987), pp. 22-23.
8. Anne Morrow Lindbergh, *Gift from the Sea*, 1955. Reprint (New York: Pantheon Books, 1975), p. 58.
9. Joan Borysenko, *Minding the Body, Mending the Mind* (Reading, Mass.: Addison-Wesley Publishing, 1987), p. 20.
10. Mihaly Csikszentmihalyi, *Flow—The Psychology of Optimal Experience* (New York: Harper & Row, 1990), p. 169.
11. Og Mandino, *The Greatest Salesman in the World Part II—The End of the Story* (New York: Bantam Books, 1988), pp. 97-98.
12. Taylor, *Positive Illusions*, pp. 46-47.
13. "Body and Soul," *Newsweek*, November 7, 1988, p. 89.

14. David Spiegel, Helena C. Kraemer, Joan R. Bloom, and Ellen Gottheil, "Effect of Psychosocial Treatment on Survival of Patients with Metastic Breast Cancer," *The Lancet*, October 14, 1989, pp. 889-91.

15. Fawzy I. Fawzy, Margaret E. Kemeny, Nancy W. Fawzy, Robert Elashoff, Donald Morton, Norman Cousins, and John L. Fahey, "A Structured Psychiatric Intervention for Cancer Patients," *Archives of General Psychiatry* 47 (August 1990), pp. 729-35.

16. Bill Moyers, *Healing and the Mind* (Garden City, N.Y.: Doubleday Publishing, 1993), pp. 195-97. Interview with Margaret Kemeny. Researchers hoped to discover positive emotions' link to increased immune cell production. They were surprised to learn that the expressions of sadness also yielded short-term increases in natural killer cells. Researchers may discover that expression of emotions has beneficial physiological implications and that suppression of emotions suppresses immune function. But as Kemeny points out, "We're in an area of science that we're really only beginning to understand." (p. 199).

17. Donald L. Kanter and Philip H. Mirvis, *The Cynical Americans* (San Francisco: Jossey-Bass, 1989), pp. 10-11. The authors' research shows that 43% of the American working population fits the profile of a cynic. This group believes that lying, putting on a "false face," and doing whatever it takes to make money are all part of human nature. Forty-one percent of the working population was found to be basically upbeat about people. The remaining 16% was labeled as wary, tending to slightly agree or slightly disagree with statements listed in the authors' cynicism index.

18. Covey, *The Seven Habits*. The author describes proactive people as creating their own weather.

Appendix

1. Walter Coleman, telephone interview, January 8, 1993.

INDEX

Switchboard operator, 23-26

T

T.G.I. Friday's restaurant, 20
Take-a-number system, 7-8
Talking in conflict resolution, 95
Talk time standards, 18
Tandy Corporation, 33-34
Taurus; *see* Ford Taurus
Tavello, Jill, 109
Tavris, Carol, 65
Taylor, Shelley, 134
TCI Cablevision, 30
Team interviewing, 111
Teamwork, 85-86
Teen Talk Barbie, 76
Telephone calls by customers, 5, 8-19
Telephone greetings, 26-28
Thinly disguised contempt, (TDC), 69
Thorpe, Jim, 131
Time management, 1-19, 132
Tires, 87-88
Toll-free numbers, 17, 77-79
Towson Town Center, 22
Transactional analysis, 92
Transferring calls, 28-29, 106
Tritten, Ray, 88
Trust of the customer, 47
Twinbrook Insurance Agency, 28
Twinbrook technique, 28-29
Type A personality, 104

U

University of California, Berkeleym, 135
University of California, Los Angeles, 135
University of Notre Dame, 110

V

Veraldi, Lewis C., 75
VideO-carts, 4
Voice mail, 85, 103-105

W

Waers, Bill, 78, 109
Wait time standard, 4-5
Waiting, 4-8
   in line, 1-4
Walking by automation, 13-15
Walk-up traffic, 8
Wall of Fame, 118
Wal-Mart, 22
Walt Disney Company, 40
Walton, Sam, 22
Warner Cable, 124
Weather channel, 4
Whirlpool Corporation, 77-78, 109-110, 138
WIIFM behavior, 116
Wingmasters, 4
Wizard of Oz response, 41
WordPerfect Corporation, 4, 16
Working the room, 76-77
Written communication in conflict resolution, 94

Other excellent resources available from Irwin Professional Publishing . . .

THE NEW OWNER

Making the Transition from Employee to Employer
Eric R. Voth and Ron Myers
(263 pages) ISBN: 1-55623-965-3

For employees planning on owning their own businesses, new business owners, and managers of small- to medium-sized businesses, this guide offers a prescription for making all efforts run as smoothly as possible. You'll also find:

- How to let competent managers make many of the day-to-day decisions, leaving you free to keep the business on course.
- A customer service "report card" and goal planning sheet, to ensure quality service and the success of your management efforts.
- A small business owner's prescription to freedom.

SERVICE AMERICA!

Doing Business in the New Economy
Karl Albrecht and Ron Zemke
(203 pages) ISBN: 0-87094-659-5

More than 250,000 copies sold! This classic service primer shows you how to make quality service an imperative in your organization and increase your profits through customer loyalty.

401 GREAT LETTERS

Kim Komando
(432 pages) ISBN: 1-55623-835-5   (W/ 5-1/4" disk)
ISBN: 1-55623-833-9   (book only)

This book of letters transcends all previously published books of this nature by providing full-in-the-blank templates for over 400 real-life, real-issues letters. The accompanying disk, containing ready made templates, is a real time-saver!

THE CREATIVE COMMUNICATOR

399 Tools to Communicate Commitment without Boring People to Death!

Barbara A. Glanz

(192 pages)   ISBN: 1-55623-832-0

Provides models, guidelines, and ideas that creatively and innovatively communicate a company's commitment to quality. Successful companies and individuals share inventive ideas for communicating in creative ways. Covers all of the Malcolm Baldrige Award criteria.

Available at fine bookstores and libraries everywhere.